THE WAY
OF
HOLINESS

KENNETH F. W. PRIOR

INTER-VARSITY PRESS

© INTER-VARSITY PRESS

Inter-Varsity Fellowship
39 Bedford Square, London WC1B 3EY

First Edition	*March 1967*
Reprinted	*April 1972, July 1974*

ISBN 0 85110 360 X

Biblical quotations are from the Revised Standard Version
unless otherwise stated.

Made and printed in England by
COMPTON PRINTING LIMITED
London and Aylesbury

CONTENTS

PREFACE

NO-ONE can pretend that the subject of this book is an easy one. To add to the confusion of the ordinary Christian many theories have been advanced and experiences claimed. There is only one remedy, and that is to return to Scripture and find out what it teaches. We must use terms in exactly the same sense as Scripture uses them and ruthlessly avoid expressions that find no place in the Word of God. Experiences must be interpreted in the light of Scripture and not vice versa. Considerable care must also be taken with analogies, because no analogy, no matter how satisfying an explanation it may seem to provide, will do unless the point at issue is clearly seen in Scripture. God has not left the teaching of His Word to be improved upon by human ingenuity!

All this is precisely the purpose of this book. In view of the many misunderstandings on this subject, I have not shrunk from exposing as error anything that seems to conflict with Scripture, and inevitably a large amount of space has had to be devoted to this unavoidable task. I sincerely hope that doing this will not cost me any friends! In some cases I am criticizing views that I once held myself but have been compelled to relinquish in the light of Scripture.

I gladly acknowledge the help of many teachers. In particular, the writings of such giants as John Owen, J. C. Ryle, B. B. Warfield, Handley Moule and T. C. Hammond have been constantly at my side. I am grateful for many helpful suggestions received in the preparation of this book from Eric Alexander, R. C. Lucas, Derek Swann and Leon Morris.

K. F. W. P.

CHAPTER I

THE WAY OF HOLINESS

THE life God plans for His people is described by Isaiah as 'the way of holiness' (Is. 35: 8, AV). But what is holiness? For many people, the word, if it conveys anything at all, revives memories of stained-glass windows depicting pale and unhealthy-looking faces with bones clearly visible under a thin layer of flesh! It calls to mind hair shirts and other things designed to ensure that life is not too enjoyable, and always present, of course, is the inevitable halo to underline the utter impracticability of the whole idea.

But is this really what the Bible means by the word 'holiness'? Far from it. The holy men of the Bible are miles removed from such popular misconceptions. Instead of their being weak and anaemic, we find they are often tough with sunburnt faces, like Elijah, John the Baptist and, be it reverently suggested, our Lord Himself. Instead of being miserable, they are full of joy, like Paul, the great apostle to the Gentiles, whose happiness was so deep and lasting that he could sing even in a filthy Roman prison, where he had been committed for the 'crime' of preaching the gospel. Instead of being distinguished from ordinary men by an unearthly halo, the early Christians mixed with all types of humanity, from the publicans and sinners of the Gospels, and the 'fatherless and widows' of the Epistle of James, to 'the saints . . . of Caesar's household' (Phil. 4: 22).

Holiness, when rightly understood, is an attractive quality, not something forbidding and inhuman. James Philip rightly observes: 'The greatest saints of God have been characterized, not by haloes and an atmosphere of distant unapproachability, but by their humanity. They have been intensely human and lovable people with a twinkle in their eyes. One has only to read the biographies of men like Moody, or Spurgeon, or

7

Hudson Taylor, to see how true this is.'[1] Holiness, then, is a practical concept, and has to do with our present earthly life, rather than with some future, heavenly existence ('glorification' is the word for that). The holy person is one who reveals here and now a very real sense of purpose and victory. C. H. Spurgeon, that great nineteenth-century preacher, once said: 'It would be a great pity if in the process of being qualified for the next life, we become disqualified for this; but it is not so. It would be a very strange thing if, in order to be fit for the company of angels, we should grow unfit to associate with men; but it is not so. It would be a singular circumstance if those who speak of heaven have nothing to say concerning the way thither; but it is not so. . . . True religion has as much to do with this world as with the world to come; it is always urging us onward to the higher and better life; but it does so by processes and precepts which fit us worthily to spend our days while here below.'[2] Now it is with these 'processes and precepts', as Spurgeon calls them, that the doctrine of sanctification is concerned.

Although in English there are two groups of words, 'holy' and 'holiness' on the one hand and 'sanctify', 'sanctification' and 'saint' on the other, in both Hebrew and Greek the adjective, noun and verb which these words translate are all derived from one root.[3] Now Christian theology has always regarded these words as expressing one of the basic doctrines underlying the Christian life. Sanctification has been made a kind of heading under which various aspects of the Christian life have been placed. Growth in grace, victory over sin, and the present inward work of the Holy Spirit in the heart of the believer, transforming his nature, are among them. Many references in Scripture are quoted in this connection, even though the passages may not contain either of these words. If we want a clear summary of the range of truth in-

---

[1] J. Philip, *Christian Maturity* (IVF, 1964), p. 70.
[2] C. H. Spurgeon, *The Treasury of the Bible*, III, p. 277.
[3] In the New Testament there are two additional Greek adjectives occasionally used for 'holy'.

cluded in sanctification, it is hard to better the definition given in the Westminster Catechism, the statement of doctrine officially held by the Presbyterian churches. Sanctification is said to be 'the work of God's free grace, whereby we are renewed in the whole man after the image of God, and are enabled more and more to die unto sin, and live unto righteousness'.

All this is in keeping with biblical usage. In 1 Thessalonians 5, for example, Paul gives a number of directives for Christian living, and then summarizes in the words, 'may the God of peace himself sanctify you wholly' (1 Thes. 5: 23). To quote John Owen's comment on this verse, 'The reason hereof is, because all the graces and duties which he had enjoined, belonged to their sanctification.'[1] Peter, too, uses the idea of holiness as a basic factor of the Christian life which finds its application in the various commands of God. He bids us 'Be holy yourselves in all your conduct' (1 Pet. 1: 15). Just as 'uncleanness' is a general word for the life of sin, so 'holiness' is the opposite; it includes all the positive virtue that God intends.

Holiness, therefore, is the characteristic mark of a Christian. It is one of the chief purposes of his election, for 'he chose us in him before the foundation of the world, that we should be holy and blameless before him' (Eph. 1: 4). Or, as Paul put it when writing to the Romans, 'Whom he foreknew he also predestined to be conformed to the image of his Son' (Rom. 8: 29). Moreover, it is commanded for every Christian without distinction. It is to the rank and file of the church and not to the members of some special religious order that the apostle writes: 'This is the will of God, your sanctification' (1 Thes. 4: 3).

This misconception—that holiness is intended for an *élite* within the church—often goes with the stained-glass window ideas. It is an attitude usually associated with the Roman Catholic church, but it is by no means confined to it. Are not many Christians dominated by a tacit assumption that there

[1] J. Owen, *On the Holy Spirit* (1674), p. 220.

are two standards of Christian commitment, one for missionaries and a lower one for 'ordinary' Christians? We expect missionaries to sacrifice money, earthly comforts and even marriage in pursuit of their calling. But it is different for the rest of us. Or is it? Is this a biblical attitude? Certainly not. Nowhere in Scripture is there any suggestion of such a double standard. When Paul, for example, was addressing the Christians at Corinth, he did not say: 'Saint Paul to the Christians at Corinth', but 'Paul, called by the will of God to be an apostle . . . to those sanctified in Christ Jesus, called to be saints' (1 Cor. 1: 1, 2). He did not use the name 'saint' exclusively for himself and those like him, but applied it to all the members of the church in Corinth. And, as the rest of the Epistle makes clear, this included some who had not progressed far in the life of sanctification. All alike are called to be saints.

The pursuit of holiness, then, is one of the supreme quests in which a Christian is to be engaged. We are not primarily to seek happiness, although this will come our way as a by-product, as Jesus Himself promised: 'Happy are those who are hungry and thirsty for goodness, for they will be fully satisfied!' (Mt. 5: 6, J. B. Phillips). Holiness, not happiness, must come first, for it is essential to salvation. 'Strive for . . . the holiness without which no one will see the Lord' (Heb. 12: 14). No-one who is careless about this is entitled to any assurance of salvation. Indeed, it would be an unwarranted presumption to imagine that we can enjoy forgiveness and eternal life without any intention to be made holy. So any professing Christian who is unconcerned about the truths faced in this book ought in all seriousness to heed the advice of Paul: 'Examine yourselves, to see whether you are holding to your faith. Test yourselves' (2 Cor. 13: 5).

CHAPTER II

THE HOLINESS OF GOD

ANY study in the doctrine of sanctification ought to begin with the holiness of God. Holiness is primarily a divine attribute and is referred to in the Old Testament more than all the other attributes of God put together. It is because God is holy that He commands His creatures to be holy. The command, 'You shall be holy; for I the Lord your God am holy' (Lv. 19: 2) is the basis on which this doctrine is built in the Bible. God first reveals Himself to His people as essentially holy; then He proceeds to demand the same from them. We cannot stress too strongly that the supreme motive is not because holiness is the way of happiness or peace of mind, but because it is an obligation placed upon us by One who is Himself holy.

But holiness in the Christian believer is not only the result of a command. If it were, there would be small likelihood of us sinners becoming in any degree holy. A Christian's holiness arises out of his relationship with a holy God. We are 'partakers of the divine nature' (2 Pet. 1: 4) or, as the writer to the Hebrews puts it, we 'share his holiness' (Heb. 12: 10). In other words, holiness is not only commanded by God's law, but is made available to men by His grace.

This recognition of the divine holiness as the essential background to the sanctification of the believer is assumed in the Westminster Catechism definition, which describes it as a process of being 'renewed in the whole man after the image of God'. In sanctification God is fulfilling His original creative purpose, which was to 'make man in our image' (Gn. 1: 26). His ultimate aim is nothing short of making men like Himself. To use a kindred term, sanctification is concerned with promoting 'godliness', a word which has sadly disappeared from the vocabulary of many Christians.

What do we mean when we describe God as holy? To define this exactly is no easy matter. Mercifully, a complete investigation into the various definitions which have been advanced is beyond the scope of this book. Instead, we shall content ourselves with a grasp of the basic idea, bearing in mind that our ultimate objective is a practical one, to discover the way of holy living that God intends for His people. First of all, what is the literal meaning of the words 'holy' and 'sanctify'?

Unlike so many words employed in the Bible, they are exclusively religious words, and are used only where God and His will for the lives of His people are in view. Although there is no absolute certainty about the meaning of the Hebrew root, the majority opinion is that it is a Semitic one and means 'to cut', and so conveys the idea of 'to separate' or 'to set apart'. So when God is described as 'holy' it means that He is separated from His creation and exalted above it. He is, to quote Isaiah 57: 15, 'the high and lofty One who inhabits eternity, whose name is Holy'. Furthermore, He is distinct from His creatures; no-one may be compared with Him. Again, we use the words of Isaiah: 'To whom then will you compare me, that I should be like him? says the Holy One' (Is. 40: 25). It is this quality of holiness which false gods lack, as Moses recognized when he exclaimed: 'Who is like thee, O Lord, among the gods? Who is like thee, majestic in holiness?' (Ex. 15: 11).

Although for convenience the holiness of God is often grouped in theological textbooks with His so-called 'moral attributes', such as His righteousness, love and mercy, this is really a kind of master-attribute which includes all the others in their perfection. For is it not God's perfect goodness, His unquenchable zeal for righteousness, the boundlessness of His love, the limitless power which He wields, and His infinite wisdom and understanding which render Him so utterly different from His creatures and elevate Him over them? To say He is holy is just another way of saying He is God. Indeed, in the Old Testament, God is sometimes simply designated 'the Holy One'.

All this was emphasized in Rudolf Otto's important book, translated into English under the title *The Idea of the Holy*,[1] which has had such a salutary effect on our thinking on this subject. It shows that holiness is no mere negative concept, but the most essential ingredient in the very nature of God, for which Otto coined the word 'the Numinous'. It produces a sense that one is in the presence of something strange and unfamiliar. This is how C. S. Lewis explains it: 'Those who have not met this term may be introduced to it by the following device. Suppose you were told there was a tiger in the next room: you would know that you were in danger and would probably feel fear. But if you were told "There is a ghost in the next room", and believed it, you would feel, indeed, what is often called fear, but of a different kind. It would not be based on the knowledge of danger, for no one is primarily afraid of what a ghost may do to him, but of the mere fact that it is a ghost. It is "uncanny" rather than dangerous, and the special kind of fear it excites may be called Dread. With the Uncanny one has reached the fringes of the Numinous. Now suppose that you were told simply "There is a mighty spirit in the room", and believed it. Your feelings would then be even less like the mere fear of danger: but the disturbance would be profound. You would feel wonder and a certain shrinking—a sense of inadequacy to cope with such a visitant and of prostration before it—an emotion which might be expressed in Shakespeare's words "Under it my genius is rebuked". This feeling may be described as awe, and the object which excites it as the *Numinous*.'[2]

THE HOLINESS OF GOD AND SIN

Although we have not yet seen in the idea of holiness any ethical content, Christianity certainly teaches that one of the ways in which God is separated from His creatures and

[1] R. Otto, *The Idea of the Holy*, translated by J. W. Harvey (OUP, 1946).
[2] C. S. Lewis, *The Problem of Pain* (Bles, Fontana, 1940), pp. 4f.

elevated above them is with regard to their sin. But not every religion recognizes this. As Bishop Stephen Neill points out: 'The idea that holiness could exist without ethical virtue has become completely strange to us. It is well to remember that this may be true of us, but it is not everywhere and universally true. In India, for example, both religion and ethics exist, but the unbreakable connection between them has never yet been made. It is possible for an earnest Hindu to seek contact with the "holy" . . . to attain to a very deep sense of the "numinous", to feel that he has been in touch with the *mysterium tremendum*, and yet not to be convinced that such an experience need be in any way related to a demand for ethical righteousness, or that the experience, if attained, need necessarily have any direct effect on his moral conduct in the future.'[1]

The application of holiness to sin is, however, clearly recognized in the Bible. The prophet Habakkuk, for example, having addressed God as 'my Holy One' continues, 'Thou who art of purer eyes than to behold evil and canst not look on wrong' (Hab. 1: 12 f.). With these words in mind, Professor R. A. Finlayson has described holiness as 'a general term for the moral excellence of God, and His freedom from all moral limitations in His moral perfection . . . a declaration expressive of the moral sensitiveness of God, shrinking from all evil and sin'.[2]

All this means that God cannot compromise with sin in any form. He must demand conformity with His moral laws, and anyone who would have dealings with Him must be pure in thought, word and deed. 'Who shall ascend the hill of the Lord? And who shall stand in his holy place?' asks the psalmist. Back comes the reply: 'He who has clean hands and a pure heart, who does not lift up his soul to what is false, and does not swear deceitfully' (Ps. 24: 3, 4). To summarize in the words of Berkhof: 'This ethical holiness of God may be defined as that perfection of God, in virtue of which He eter-

[1] S. C. Neill, *Christian Holiness* (Lutterworth, 1960), p. 19.
[2] R. A. Finlayson, *The Holiness of God* (Pickering and Inglis, 1955), p. 4.

nally wills and maintains His own moral excellence, abhors sin, and demands purity in His moral creatures.'[1]

When men fail to fulfil these requirements, God's holiness demands that He expresses His displeasure in wrath and judgment (see, *e.g.*, Is. 5: 16). It is not surprising, then, if men faced with such a God sense their own sin and unworthiness. They will be like Isaiah who, having seen the Lord 'high and lifted up', and heard the 'Holy, holy, holy' of the seraphim, confessed: 'Woe is me! For I am lost; for I am a man of unclean lips, and I dwell in the midst of a people of unclean lips; for my eyes have seen the King, the Lord of hosts!' (Is. 6: 5).

MAN'S RESPONSE TO GOD'S HOLINESS

What is the bearing of all this on our subject? It has a very profound bearing, for not only does it help to show us what holiness is, but it also gives us the supreme ground for our holiness. If God's people are to become holy, it is essential they should face the challenge of God's holiness. They will 'sanctify the Lord of hosts himself' (Is. 8: 13, AV), that is, they will acknowledge Him to be holy. This is what is expressed in the familiar words of the Lord's Prayer, 'hallowed be Thy Name', for 'hallow' is the same word as 'sanctify' in Greek. When Peter employs these words from Isaiah he does so with some significant modifications. Not only does he apply them to Christ, but he significantly adds 'in your hearts' (1 Pet. 3: 15). We are to recognize the holiness of God, not merely by the profession of our lips, but in the submission of our hearts.[2] If a Christian is to avoid compromising his standards in the midst of opposition, then from the very centre of his being there must be this awesome attitude towards God in His holiness.

Now the word used in Scripture for this attitude is 'fear'. As our quotation from Isaiah 8: 13 (AV) says: 'Sanctify the Lord of hosts himself; and let him be your fear, and let him be your

---

[1] L. Berkhof, *Systematic Theology* (Banner of Truth, 1959), p. 74.

[2] *E.g.*, Is. 29:13, where again the word 'honour' is the word translated 'sanctify' elsewhere.

dread.' This is no slavish, cowering emotion but the healthy attitude of awe and reverence which befits the holiness of God. It is the 'reverence and godly fear' which the writer to the Hebrews sees as a necessary accompaniment of the kind of service God requires (Heb. 12: 28, AV). If holiness is the supreme attribute of God, then reverence must be correspondingly paramount in the manner in which His people are to regard Him. This reverence is significantly defined by the psychologist McDougall as 'the religious emotion *par excellence*; few merely human powers are capable of exciting reverence, this blend of wonder, fear, gratitude, and negative self-feeling'.[1]

Now the fear of the Lord has a great deal to do with the way in which a Christian lives. Paul, for example, urges his readers to 'make holiness perfect in the fear of God' (2 Cor. 7: 1). The book of Proverbs is full of teaching about the practical importance of the fear of God as the following quotations demonstrate:

'The fear of the Lord is the beginning of knowledge' (1: 7);
'The fear of the Lord is hatred of evil' (8: 13);
'In the fear of the Lord one has strong confidence' (14: 26);
'The fear of the Lord is a fountain of life' (14: 27);
'By the fear of the Lord a man avoids evil' (16: 6).

Yet the importance of reverence and fear towards God in relation to the whole subject of sanctification is not always given the recognition it deserves. Surely, one of the reasons in these days for low moral standards is the lack of awareness of the majesty and holiness of God and of our accountability towards Him. To a certain degree the same deficiencies can be seen amongst professing Christians. One of the marks of spiritual decline is that 'there is no fear of God before his eyes' (Ps. 36: 1). Instead man fills himself with confidence in his own sufficiency, which is the complete antithesis of holiness.

[1] W. McDougall, *An Introduction to Social Psychology* (Methuen, 1908), p. 132.

CHAPTER III

HOLINESS IN MEN

AS we have seen, it is because God is holy that He calls upon His people to be holy. What does it mean then for men to be holy, and so to share in what is essentially a divine attribute? To pass from the holiness of the Almighty and Eternal God to holiness in finite and earthbound man is a big jump. Let us therefore use what Scripture teaches about the holiness of places and objects as a kind of stepping-stone for our understanding.

HOLINESS OF PLACES AND OBJECTS

Places may be described as holy when they become the scene of an awareness of the presence of the holy God and therefore the occasion of awe and wonder. Such places become unapproachable because they are set apart and different from others. Most people are barred from drawing near at all, while those who may, are entitled to do so only on certain conditions. Take, for example, the regulations governing the entering of the high priest into the holy of holies once a year in the Temple.

A helpful example of a holy place is the burning bush where Moses was told 'the place on which you are standing is holy ground' (Ex. 3: 5). The place had become so associated with God Himself that it, too, was holy and therefore unapproachable. Even Moses was allowed to draw near only after the removal of his shoes. Like the holiness of God Himself, so the holiness of objects and places has both positive and negative aspects. Positively, the places are set apart for God, while negatively, any who would mar them must be excluded.

There are also many examples in the Old Testament of objects being regarded as holy. We may cite the vessels and furnishings of the Tabernacle and the Temple (see, *e.g.*, Ex. 40: 10 f.). Here again there are the same two aspects. Positively, they were set apart for the service and worship of God, while negatively, they were set apart from all other use and had to be ceremonially cleansed before they were worthy of the purpose for which they were intended.

As an example of days being holy we may choose the Sabbath.[1] It was to be kept holy because it was a day specially belonging to God. And if the day was to be devoted to God it meant that it had to be freed from the activities with which people were occupied on the remaining six days.

HOLINESS IN MEN

These examples help us to understand one aspect of holiness in men. When they were appointed to special office under the old economy they, too, were 'sanctified'. Here the word is not being used in any ethical sense. It was not that they had reached some particular degree of moral attainment and were necessarily any less sinful than others. Indeed, one could be a sacred person yet completely lacking in spiritual life and character, and this is amply demonstrated in the Old Testament. The New Testament has similar ways of speaking when it refers to 'holy prophets' and 'holy apostles'. It is in this sense that we speak of the apostles as 'Saint Paul', 'Saint John' and so on. They were set apart for the special office of being an apostle, which for them involved, among other things, the privilege and responsibility of being the human writers of Holy Scripture.[2] It was no doubt in a similar sense that our Lord applied this to Himself when He prayed, 'for their sakes I sanctify myself, that they also might be sanctified through the truth' (Jn. 17: 19, AV). He was not purging Himself from any evil which had previously been present, but He was setting Himself apart

[1] Incidentally, it is in connection with the Sabbath that the word 'holy' is first used in Scripture (Gn. 2: 3).

[2] For examples of this use of 'holy' see Lk. 1: 70; Eph. 3: 5; 2 Pet. 1: 21.

for the work of redemption, which meant both positive dedication to all that it involved and separation from everything that would hinder.

Now although holiness may have the particular reference just mentioned, it is also laid as an obligation on all God's people. When Peter puts before his readers the challenge of God's holiness, he addresses it not just to those called to special office but to the entire congregation to whom he is writing (1 Pet. 1: 15, 16). Just as 'I am holy' summarizes all that goes to make God what He is, so the command 'You shall be holy' lays before God's people what is to be their distinctive characteristic. Just as a place when associated with God becomes holy, with all the precautions and demands which that makes, so must a person who would have dealings with the 'Holy One'. Little wonder the Hebrew Christians are challenged to 'strive for . . . holiness without which no one will see the Lord' (Heb. 12: 14). Indeed, when we consider the Final Judgment we see that in the last analysis there are only two classes of people, the holy and the unholy. Notice the finality with which this is expressed in the last chapter of the Bible: 'Let the evildoer still do evil, and the filthy still be filthy, and the righteous still do right, and the holy still be holy' (Rev. 22: 11).

We have already seen that holiness has both negative and positive implications. Let us now look at these again.

The negative aspect of holiness
The first reaction men show when challenged by God's holiness and the demands it makes upon them is surely an awareness of their unworthiness. The holiness of God has been likened to a bright, searching light which ruthlessly shows up all that is impure and unclean. When Isaiah had his vision of the holiness of God he was immediately prostrated with a sense of his own sin. As he tried to open his mouth he was aware that the very lips with which he spoke were morally unclean. He saw the hopelessness of his position and all he could say for himself was 'Woe is me!' (Is. 6: 5). Peter seems to have had a similar experience. Having seen our Lord at work and heard

something of His teaching, he must have caught a glimpse of God's holiness expressed in the perfection with which Jesus went about His task, for we are told, 'He fell down at Jesus' knees, saying, "Depart from me, for I am a sinful man, O Lord" ' (Lk. 5: 8). This reaction to God's holiness is the only one that befits a sinner, and if, in spite of our sin, we are to be the people of a holy God, then we are impelled to share His abhorrence of our sin. The call to holiness is a call to come out on God's side of the gulf that separates Him from our sin. This will mean separating ourselves from everything that is sinful and unworthy, for cleanliness in thought, word and deed is demanded of all those who would approach God.

Holiness is demanded of men when they are praying, for prayer is to be pursued 'lifting holy hands' (1 Tim. 2: 8). When Isaiah had censured God's people for their lack of holiness, he went on to expose the uselessness of their prayers while in that condition: 'When you spread forth your hands, I will hide my eyes from you; even though you make many prayers, I will not listen; your hands are full of blood' (Is. 1: 15). The remedy therefore in the subsequent verses is obvious: 'Wash yourselves; make yourselves clean; remove the evil of your doings from before my eyes; cease to do evil, learn to do good; seek justice, correct oppression; defend the fatherless, plead for the widow' (Is. 1: 16, 17).

We have to remember, too, that the life of holiness has to be lived in the midst of a world that has been marred and ruined by sin. A Christian's holiness will mean therefore that his way of life will often be utterly different from those around him. This point is repeatedly made in the Old Testament, and it was on the ground of holiness that they were forbidden to follow the customs of the tribes around them (Dt. 12: 1-19). They were not, for example, allowed to take wives of pagan tribes. In the New Testament the standard is no lower. Christians are to maintain the same distinctiveness as their Old Testament counterparts. Addressing Christians living amidst the corruptions of a typical pagan city of the ancient world, Paul writes: 'Therefore come out from them, and be separate from them, says the Lord, and touch nothing unclean; then I will welcome you' (2 Cor. 6: 17).

In view of all this, any study in sanctification must be largely occupied with sin and how it is overcome. Making holiness perfect involves us in cleansing ourselves from 'every defilement of body and spirit' (2 Cor. 7: 1). So in the following chapters we shall be considering the nature of sin, the extent of the damage it has caused, and God's answer to it. Before we do this, however, we must describe the positive side of holiness, for this is something of which we must never lose sight.

The positive aspect of holiness

Holiness is something much more than just avoiding sin and getting rid of our corrupt nature. It goes far beyond simply undoing the effect of the Fall, as an old couplet shows:

> 'In Christ the sons of Adam boast
> More blessings than their father lost.'

In the matter of character, this involves reflecting the very image of Jesus Christ Himself. God's purpose is that we shall be 'conformed to the image of his Son' (Rom. 8: 29). Elsewhere Paul expresses the same idea thus: 'We all, with unveiled face, beholding the glory of the Lord, are being changed into his likeness from one degree of glory to another; for this comes from the Lord who is Spirit' (2 Cor. 3: 18). Now Adam may have enjoyed many of God's blessings before he fell. But, as the couplet quoted above implies, in his untried state he came a long way short in his experience of all that God ultimately intends for His people.

Virtue in the New Testament is always positive. It is not only a matter of avoiding sins but exercising the positive virtues in their place. Instead of yielding our members 'to impurity and greater and greater iniquity', we are to yield our members to 'righteousness for sanctification' (Rom. 6: 19). Paul brings this out very fully in his list of qualities in Ephesians 4: 25–32. Notice that each sin is to be substituted by a positive virtue. Instead of lying, there is to be truth. Instead of stealing, there is to be work and generosity. Evil talk is to be replaced by that which is edifying, while bitterness, wrath and anger are to be renounced in favour of kindness and forgiveness one to another. In short, to summarize it in Paul's own way, we are not only to put off the old man but also to put on the new.

It is clear, then, that sanctification and holiness must result in good works. It is a matter of being 'holy yourselves in all your conduct' (1 Pet. 1: 15). To use the language employed by our Lord, a sound tree must produce good fruit just as a bad tree produces evil fruit (Mt. 7: 16 ff.). This is an essential result of abiding in Christ, for as our Lord Himself claimed, 'He who abides in me, and I in him, he it is that bears much fruit' (Jn. 15: 5). So sanctification is much more than a spiritual experience. Indeed, there can be a subtle piece of self-deception in this matter. Experiences of 'blessing' can be a substitute for practical holiness. It has not been unknown for Christians to have claimed some great spiritual experience or attainment and yet be just as selfish, bad-tempered or indisciplined as before. Let us remember that the Holy Spirit produces fruit which includes the much-needed virtues of 'love, joy, peace, patience, kindness, goodness, faithfulness, gentleness, self-control' (Gal. 5: 22, 23).

It would be a mistake, however, to imagine that holiness is just another word for moral improvement. If it were, holiness would be within reach of unregenerate men. Holiness is based on a relationship between the sinner and God, and the Christian seeks to be holy in order to please Him and to glorify His name. Works of holiness spring out of the desire to obey God's will and to please Him.

Holiness also includes another very positive factor which shows that it is much more than moral endeavour. Like the vessels in the Temple, we have been purified for a purpose, for, 'If any one purifies himself from what is ignoble, then he will be a vessel for noble use, consecrated and useful to the master of the house, ready for any good work' (2 Tim. 2: 21). The same positive emphasis is also made in the following

verses on consecration which are often quoted and used in
addresses on this subject: 'I appeal to you therefore, brethren,
by the mercies of God, to present your bodies as a living sacrifice, holy and acceptable to God, which is your spiritual worship. Do not be conformed to this world but be transformed
by the renewal of your mind, that you may prove what is the
will of God, what is good and acceptable and perfect' (Rom.
12: 1, 2). Again there are reminiscences of the worship in the
Temple. When our bodies are consecrated to God, like the
animals sacrificed in Old Testament worship, they become the
exclusive property of God, to be used for His service. Our
minds also are included, for they are to be renewed with the
positive purpose of proving what is the will of God.

CHAPTER IV

SIN

'HE that wishes to attain right views about Christian holiness must begin by examining the vast and solemn subject of sin. He must dig down very low if he would build high. A mistake here is most mischievous. Wrong views about holiness are generally traceable to wrong views about human corruption. . . . If a man does not realize the dangerous nature of his soul's disease, you cannot wonder if he is content with false or imperfect remedies.'[1] So Bishop Ryle began his volume of papers on holiness. Undoubtedly he was right. Shallow views about holiness and sanctification have nearly always been accompanied by inadequate doctrines of sin. But the Bible gives a very serious diagnosis of the sin from which we need to be delivered. Nowhere does it play down its strength or the tenacity with which it clings to men. So we, too, ought to consider this topic before proceeding any further.

WHAT IS SIN?

To this question we can give a simple and direct answer: any thought, word or deed is a sin which is not in conformity with God's law. This is in accordance with the clear statement of Scripture, 'Sin is lawlessness' (1 Jn. 3: 4). Notice that God's law is the standard by which we are judged. Sin is not simply a failure to live according to our ability, but a failure to conform to God's revealed will and purpose. The world sometimes tells us to do our best, with the assurance that no man can do more. This may be so, but our best is still a long way short of God's commandment and it is His standard which really counts.

[1] J. C. Ryle, *Holiness* (James Clarke, 1952), p. 1.

Here, of course, we have one of the supreme purposes of God's law and in these days when, in some circles, it is fashionable to deprecate law as the basis for morality, it is important to consider it. The law is intended to reveal sin in its true character. When Paul asks the all-important question, 'Why then the law?' (*i.e.*, in view of the gospel covenant with Abraham which the law cannot disannul), he answers, 'It was added because of transgressions.' The New English Bible surely brings out what was in the apostle's mind by rendering this last sentence, 'It was added to make wrongdoing a legal offence' (Gal. 3: 19). God's law, then, shows us that we are sinners; as Paul points out again and again in the Epistle to the Romans, 'through the law comes knowledge of sin' (Rom. 3: 20), and 'Where there is no law there is no transgression' (Rom. 4: 15). (Compare also Rom. 5: 13 and 1 Tim. 1: 8 ff.) As E. F. Kevan pointed out: 'Legal concepts of sin are not on any account to be dismissed as artificial: rather are they the necessary expression of sin's heinousness and of the abhorrence with which God must view it. Law, therefore, does not give to sin its awful, wrath-deserving nature: it merely provides a category in which to express this terrible fact.'[1]

We must not forget, moreover, that sin applies as much to the thought-life as to words and deeds. We can commit adultery in the imagination (see Mt. 5: 27 f.), while hatred is classed with murder, the only difference being that it is committed in the heart (1 Jn. 3: 15). This is not to say that the entry of an evil thought into the mind is in itself sinful. What is wrong is the entertaining of it. We have, of course, the well-known remark of Martin Luther that no-one can prevent the birds from flying over his head, but he is responsible if the birds make a nest in his hair! Indeed, we can break every one of the ten commandments in our thoughts. The way we occupy our minds is often the key to the way we speak and act. If we are victorious in the realm of the imagination, we conquer everywhere. If, on the other hand, we are defeated here, we fight a losing battle elsewhere. The way we think

[1] E. F. Kevan, *Keep His Commandments* (Tyndale Press, 1964), p. 16.

determines our character: 'As he thinketh in his heart, so is he' (Pr. 23: 7, AV).

In addition to this, sin extends beyond the wrong things we do to the things we ought to do, but do not. To use the words of the General Confession in the Anglican Prayer Book, we sin when 'we have left undone those things which we ought to have done' as much as when 'we have done those things which we ought not to have done'. It was for 'sins of omission' that those 'on the left hand' were judged in Christ's description of the Last Judgment (Mt. 25: 31 ff.). There is no mention of acts of sin, such as lying, cheating and murder. They were sent into everlasting fire because they had neglected to give food to the hungry, drink to the thirsty, clothing to the naked, and so on. This aspect of things has frequently been forgotten by those who have made extravagant claims to sinless perfection. Even if they are innocent of all positive acts of sin (although this we find rather hard to believe!), can they honestly say they have always done all they could to relieve the needs of others? Over and above this, what about our duty towards God? Jesus sums up the first table of the law in the single command to love God with all our heart, soul and strength, and this He describes as 'the first and great commandment'. Can anyone honestly claim that he loves God in this whole-hearted, single-minded way? Paul asserts that *all* have both sinned and come short of God's glory (Rom. 3: 23); dare any of us claim to be exceptions?

Some have tried to press a distinction between conscious and unconscious sin, holding that we can be all that God requires of us as long as we are free from conscious sin. But is this really biblical? This theory is certainly not in accordance with the Old Testament, where we find Israel distinctly taught that unwitting sins rendered people unclean and called for atonement. We find this clearly stated in Leviticus, and also in Numbers (see, *e.g.*, Lv. 4; 5: 14–19; Nu. 15: 25–29). The psalmist expresses a constant concern when he prays: 'Clear thou me from hidden faults' (Ps. 19: 12). And this is just as much the teaching of the New Testament as it is of the

Old. Nowhere is anyone excused his sins on account of ignorance. The servant 'who did not know (his master's will), and did what deserved a beating' did not escape punishment (Lk. 12: 48 f.). Again we quote Bishop Ryle: 'We shall do well to remember, that when we make our own miserably imperfect knowledge and consciousness the measure of our sinfulness, we are on very dangerous ground. A deeper study of Leviticus might do us much good.'[1] Indeed, our very failure to discern what is sinful is a sign of our blindness to moral issues and our insensitivity to what is wrong.

THE CORRUPTION OF HUMAN NATURE

This brings us to the origin of sins. They do not simply originate from our upbringing, although this, of course, can play a very important part. Nor can our background receive more than part of the blame. Rather our sins spring from a corrupt nature. It is a moral disease from which man is suffering, which has affected the very centre of his being. 'The heart is deceitful above all things, and desperately corrupt' (Je. 17: 9), and it is out of that heart that all our wrongdoing springs. Our Lord drew attention to this unpleasant moral fact when He was showing the inadequacy of external ritual cleansings. He pointed out that it is not things from outside that defile a person, but rather what comes out of his own inner nature: 'What comes out of a man is what defiles a man. For from within, out of the heart of man, come evil thoughts, fornication, theft, murder, adultery, coveting, wickedness, deceit, licentiousness, envy, slander, pride, foolishness. All these evil things come from within, and they defile a man' (Mk. 7: 20–23). Elsewhere, in Luke 6, Jesus likens a man to a tree. Just as diseased fruit indicates corruption in the tree itself, so 'an evil man out of the evil treasure of his heart bringeth forth that which is evil: for of the abundance of the heart his mouth speaketh' (Lk. 6: 45, AV). All this means that as long as man's heart is diseased by sin he has a continual propensity to evil,

[1] J. C. Ryle, *Holiness* (James Clarke, 1952), p. 3.

which can make itself shown sometimes at a very early age. As the psalmist observed: 'The wicked go astray from the womb, they err from their birth, speaking lies' (Ps. 58: 3). Indeed, a man can be described as a rebel from birth (Is. 48: 8).

Here is another point at which some views of sin are hopelessly unrealistic and inadequate. Some have refused to recognize anything but external acts of sin, a view from which the Church of England has officially dissociated itself in its Articles: 'Original sin standeth not in the following of Adam, (as the Pelagians do vainly talk;) but it is the fault and corruption of the Nature of every man, that naturally is engendered of the offspring of Adam; whereby man is very far gone from original righteousness, and is of his own nature inclined to evil, so that the flesh lusteth always contrary to the spirit' (Article 9). This shallow view of sin was one of the errors of the Pharisees of our Lord's day. It was this which led to their over-emphasis of external rituals and cleansings criticized by Jesus in Mark 7. This externalizing of sin can involve a person in the subtle error of, to use James Philip's words, 'exchanging one set of sins for another, and mistaking this for deliverance'. He continues: 'It is a supreme tragedy—and very frightening—when a man, under the impression that he is being saved from sin, merely alters the pattern of sin in his life, from the less respectable and more obvious, to the less obvious and more respectable. The evil one is well satisfied to bring about such a deception.'[1]

The story of the Pharisee and the Publican is a good illustration of this all-too-common mistake. James Philip again goes straight to the heart of what this story teaches: ' . . . The real force of the parable lies in the exposure of the complete self-centredness of (the Pharisee's) life, religious though it was. It is his self-consciousness and self-absorption that obtrude throughout. The real problem of his life had never been touched; self was deeply entrenched and reigning supreme.'[2]

Many people, however, are willing to recognize that sin is basically an inward principle working contrary to God's will

[1] J. Philip, *Christian Maturity* (IVF, 1964), p. 43.   [2] *Ibid.*

and inclining the person to evil, yet they have tried to localize it. They have spoken of a person's sinful nature as something which can be readily isolated and, if necessary, eradicated. For such people the work of sanctification is a comparatively simple affair. A sinful nature can be extracted like a bad tooth—and some views of sinless perfection have virtually amounted to this. However, our condition is not as simple as this. Sin is not like a demon residing somewhere within us that can be thrown out in one piece. It is far more accurately described (again in the words of Article 9) as an 'infection of nature'; and it is an infection that 'doth remain, yea in them that are regenerated'. The Westminster Confession of the Presbyterian Churches uses similar language, reproduced almost word for word by the Baptist Confession of 1689.

To use another illustration of the same truth, our sinful nature is not like a benign growth which can be removed by a surgeon. The whole of our nature and being has been poisoned, and the remedy is better seen in terms of medicine than of surgery. So the words of the General Confession, 'there is no health in us', expose the seriousness of our condition. There is therefore no quick and sudden remedy. The work of sanctification is no simple one; there are no short cuts. It is 'that the sinful body (AV, 'whole body of sin') might be destroyed, and we might no longer be enslaved to sin' (Rom. 6: 6). God does not only have to deal with what we do, or with what we contain, but with what we are.

Let us try and avoid misunderstanding here. We are not saying that everyone is as bad as he could be. Even unregenerate men are capable of noble acts. What we must emphasize is that every part of us is to some degree infected. Nothing we do is perfect, because all our actions are tainted; when judged by God's standards even 'all our righteous deeds are like a polluted garment' (Is. 64: 6). Sin is like a drop of ink falling into a glass of water. It diffuses throughout the glass. The water may be only pale blue, but nonetheless the entire contents of the glass are coloured to some degree.

MAN'S TWOFOLD NEED

Because of his sin, man has a double need which is fully met by what God has done for him in Christ: a need arising from the guilt of sin, and from its pollution.

a. The guilt of sin

As we have seen, sin is the transgression of God's law. It is by that same law that man is judged and found guilty. As a result, man is under God's condemnation and is the object of His wrath. The penalty for infringing God's law is death, not only physical but also spiritual and eternal—'the wages of sin is death' (Rom. 6: 23)—and so God's law is also called 'the law of sin and death' (Rom. 8: 2). While a man is in this position before God not only is there no hope for him in eternity, there is equally no possibility of gaining the victory over the sinful nature for which he is condemned. Man, therefore, needs to be restored to favour with God, even though he has broken God's commandments. He needs to be pronounced 'Not Guilty' so that he can have dealings with the God he so desperately needs. In other words, he needs to be 'justified'. It is this very thing that God has done for him through the death of Jesus Christ. To describe it in Paul's words: 'Therefore, since we are justified by faith, we have peace with God through our Lord Jesus Christ' (Rom. 5: 1). And by this very fact, 'There is therefore now no condemnation for those who are in Christ Jesus' (Rom. 8: 1). To express it another way: 'The law of the Spirit of life in Christ Jesus has set me free from the law of sin and death' (Rom. 8: 2).

b. The pollution of sin

As we have already discovered, however, sin has done far more than impair man's relationship with God. It has also polluted his nature so that he is not only guilty in God's sight and under His condemnation, but also defiled and corrupt. It is as much the purpose of God to save man from this defilement as it is to remove his guilt. God does not justify a man so that he can continue in sin with impunity. 'By no means! How can we who died to sin still live in it?' (Rom. 6: 2). God does not save us in sin, but from sin, and it is with this aspect of salvation that the work of sanctification is concerned. It is to take a sinner and to set him apart from sin and for God, so that instead of serving sin he serves God. This will involve not only a change in the man's standing but also a change in his inward state and condition. The sin which has infected and corrupted him will have to be subdued, weakened and removed. It was to this need that David confessed when he prayed, 'Create in me a clean heart, O God, and put a new and right spirit within me' (Ps. 51: 10).

This is where sanctification comes in, working to purify and cleanse the heart and life of the believer until ultimately he perfectly reflects the very character of Christ Himself. It is important, however, to distinguish sanctification from justification, because confusion here has often been the cause of considerable error. In the next two chapters we shall consider the way of sanctification and the means whereby it is achieved. We shall then be in a position to see more clearly how this doctrine differs from justification.

CHAPTER V

THE MEANS OF SANCTIFICATION

FROM beginning to end sanctification is the work of God. Nobody ever made himself holy, for holiness is far beyond the reach of the natural man. This comes out impressively in 1 Thessalonians 5. After working through a long list of obligations which Paul lays upon his readers, he then says, 'May the God of peace himself sanctify you wholly' (1 Thes. 5: 23). Paul acknowledges, in this way, that although he can exhort and command his readers, and place before them the motives for obedience, it is only God who can sanctify them and so enable them to obey the commands laid down in His Word. It is, then, in the words of the Westminster Catechism, 'the work of God's free grace'.

It is important to stress this right at the beginning of the chapter, because this is another of the ways in which scriptural holiness is quite different from mere moral virtue. John Owen extols such moral virtue and says it 'is the best thing among men, that is of themselves. It far exceeds in worth, use and satisfaction, all that the honours, powers, profits, and pleasures of the world can extend unto . . . and very eminent instances of the practice of it were given in the lives of some of them, whose examples of righteousness, temperance, and equanimity in all conditions, now rise up to the shame of many called Christians, and will be called over at the last day, as an aggravation of their condemnation.' However, having said all this, Owen goes on, 'But to suppose that this moral virtue, however excellent, is that holiness of truth which believers receive by the spirit of Christ, is to debase and overthrow it, and to drive men from seeking an interest in it.'[1]

We must never lose sight of this important emphasis. There is a subtle danger of speaking of sanctification as essentially

[1] J. Owen, *On the Holy Spirit* (1674), p. 223.

coming from the effort or initiative of man. We can uncon-
sciously do this even when acknowledging our need for the
power of the Holy Spirit, by making the operation of that
power dependent upon man's surrender and consecration.
Sometimes the work of the Holy Spirit is virtually de-
personalized and 'Holy Ghost power' ('an objectionable
phrase', comments B. B. Warfield) is said to be at our disposal.
Warfield continues thus: 'God stands always helplessly by
until man calls Him into action by opening a channel into
which His energies may flow. It sounds dreadfully like turning
on the steam or the electricity. This representation is employed
not only with reference to the great matters of salvation and
sanctification, in which God's operations are "secured" (or
released) by our faith, but also with reference to every blessing
bestowed by Him. We are not only constantly exhorted to
"claim" blessings, but the enjoyment of these blessings is with
wearying iteration suspended on our "claiming" them. It is
expressly declared that God cannot bless us in any way until
we open the way for His action by an act of our own will.
Everywhere and always the initiative belongs to man; everywhere and always God's action is suspended upon man's
will. . . . It is nothing less than degrading to God to suppose
Him thus subject to the control of man and unable to move
except as man permits Him to do so, or to produce any effects
except as He is turned into the channels of their working at
man's option.'[1]

Sanctification, in Scripture, is always something which God
does. It is He who takes a man and sets him apart and then
refines his nature and challenges him to live accordingly. 'Man
does not "secure" the grace of God: the grace of God
"secures" the activities of man.'[2] What we intend to do now
is to study the manner in which God sanctifies His people and,
supremely, the agents He employs.

Some years ago the author received considerable help from

[1] B. B. Warfield, *Perfectionism* (Presbyterian and Reformed Publishing
Co., 1958), pp. 397 f.
[2] B. B. Warfield, *Perfectionism* (PRPC, 1958), p. 398.

a book by Dr. Harry Ironside, *Holiness: The False and the True*, which has unfortunately long been out of print. Dr. Ironside has three chapters devoted to the three agents of sanctification, and in this chapter we are going to take the liberty of borrowing his headings.

I. SANCTIFICATION BY THE BLOOD OF CHRIST: ETERNAL

This is one of the great themes of the Epistle to the Hebrews as the following quotations will demonstrate:

> 'For if the sprinkling of defiled persons with the blood of goats and bulls and with the ashes of a heifer sanctifies for the purification of the flesh, how much more shall the blood of Christ, who through the eternal Spirit offered himself without blemish to God, purify your conscience from dead works to serve the living God' (9: 13, 14).

> 'By that will we have been sanctified through the offering of the body of Jesus Christ once for all' (10: 10).

> 'For by a single offering he has perfected for all time those who are sanctified' (10: 14).

> 'How much worse punishment do you think will be deserved by the man who has spurned the Son of God, and profaned the blood of the covenant by which he was sanctified, and outraged the Spirit of grace?' (10: 29).

> 'So Jesus also suffered outside the gate in order to sanctify the people through his own blood' (13: 12).

An examination of these verses leads us to the following observations.

1.   The aspect of sanctification dealt with here is not an internal work of the Holy Spirit, but rather the basis on which a Christian is set apart by God. We are shown here the ground on which a Christian may regard himself as being on the Godward side of the gulf which separates God from

human sin. It is because he has been cleansed from sin and his conscience purged that the Christian is entitled to forget his past sins. He is brought into a lasting and intimate relationship with Jesus Christ, for 'he who sanctifies and those who are sanctified have all one origin. That is why he is not ashamed to call them brethren' (Heb. 2: 11). The word often used to describe this aspect of sanctification is 'positional'.

2. Sanctification is an accomplished fact depending on the sufficiency of the one offering and bloodshedding of Jesus Christ at Calvary. This is why Paul can address the Corinthian Christians as 'saints'. It is not that they had attained to any high level of sanctification in practice, but rather that they were set apart to God by virtue of Christ's death and are 'sanctified in Christ Jesus' (1 Cor. 1: 1, 2 and see also 1: 30). Sanctification, thought of in these terms, then, is certainly no experience or process subsequent to conversion. Indeed, if a Christian is asked when he was sanctified, in the sense that the Epistle to the Hebrews uses this word, the answer is not to be found in his experience at all. There is only one possible answer to such a question, and that is, 'I was sanctified two thousand years ago at Calvary!'

3. There is an eternal completeness about this aspect of sanctification (see Heb. 10: 14).

4. A person may have this status by outward association with the people of God without necessarily enjoying its inward reality. The New Testament finds an example of this in the children of Israel in the wilderness. In spite of all their outward privileges, they failed to enter the promised land because of unbelief. Here is a solemn warning for us (see, *e.g.*, Heb. 3 and 4 and compare 1 Cor. 10). Hebrews 10: 26–29 shows that a person can even have the privilege of sanctification as an outward status and yet be eternally lost.

This, incidentally, throws light on Paul's reference to the children of a believer, and even the unbelieving husband or wife, as 'holy' (1 Cor. 7: 14). By the family relationship such a person has become outwardly associated with God's people and is therefore 'sanctified by the wife' or 'sanctified by the

husband'. It was on this ground that a Christian was to continue to live with an unbelieving partner instead of forsaking
him or her and the children. Otherwise it might have seemed
that the holiness of a Christian, and especially the teaching in
the previous chapter about his body being the temple of the
Holy Ghost, demanded separation from an unbelieving partner. Furthermore, Paul sees this as an encouragement to look
for the conversion of the non-Christian husband or wife. We
hasten to add, however, that Paul is writing here of the
Christian who is already married to a non-Christian when he
is converted. There is no excuse here for a union between a
believer and an unbeliever subsequent to conversion. In such
cases the command of God is clear: 'Do not be mismated with
unbelievers' (2 Cor. 6: 14).

II. SANCTIFICATION BY THE HOLY SPIRIT: INTERNAL

Biblical theology has always recognized that sanctification has
much to do with the Holy Spirit. When holiness is ascribed to
God in the New Testament (except where the Old Testament
is being quoted), it is nearly always ascribed to the third Person of the Trinity. He is referred to as 'the Holy Spirit' more
than a hundred times. This is hardly surprising, for it is the
Holy Spirit's function to make the Christian's eternal status an
inward reality. It is He who takes the benefits of what Jesus
Christ has done on the cross and applies them to the individual
believer's heart.

It is important to be accurate here, so we will restrict ourselves to verses in the New Testament which use the actual
word 'sanctify' and attribute this work to the Holy Spirit.
First, there is the reference in 1 Corinthians 6. Paul has just
given a list of sins of which many of his readers in their pre-
Christian days had been guilty, but he then goes on to show
the difference the gospel has made to them: 'And such were
some of you. But you were washed, you were sanctified, you
were justified in the name of the Lord Jesus and in the Spirit
of our God' (1 Cor. 6: 11). We see from this statement that

the sanctifying work of the Holy Spirit is the very means whereby God's election takes effect. Those whom God has chosen are actually set apart by the Holy Spirit as He comes to indwell them. Just as the Christian for his part believes God's truth, so the Holy Spirit imparts to him this inward relationship to God. Here is another reference which will make the point even clearer: 'To the exiles . . . , chosen and destined by God the Father and sanctified by the Spirit for obedience to Jesus Christ and for sprinkling with his blood: May grace and peace be multiplied to you' (1 Pet. 1: 2). Again we see that God's electing purposes are brought to effect by the sanctifying work of the Holy Spirit; but notice the significant addition 'for obedience to Jesus Christ and for sprinkling with his blood'. In other words, the intended result of a man being set apart by God's Holy Spirit is that he should be obedient and receive the benefits of the shed blood of Jesus Christ. As A. M. Stibbs comments: 'The end in view is *obedience*—that the elect should serve the divine pleasure. Participation in such a destiny requires also the *sprinkling of the blood of Jesus Christ*.'[1] The sanctifying work of the Holy Spirit is thus fundamental to our salvation: it is the very means by which we share in the blessings of Christ's death.

Romans 15: 16 is another example of the way in which sanctification, in the New Testament, is directly attributed to the Holy Spirit. Paul speaks of the grace given him by God 'to be a minister of Christ Jesus to the Gentiles in the priestly service of the gospel of God, so that the offering of the Gentiles may be acceptable, sanctified by the Holy Spirit'. Here the apostle sees his preaching of the gospel to the Gentiles in terms of offering them up as a sacrifice to God. Yet he recognized that they could be acceptable to God only as the Holy Spirit sanctified them. Haldane remarks, 'As the sacrifices under the law were sanctified externally and typically, this figurative sacrifice is sanctified truly by the Holy Ghost. No person, then, can be acceptable to God who is not sanctified by His

[1] A. M. Stibbs, *I Peter* (Tyndale New Testament Commentary, 1959), p. 72.

Spirit.'[1] It is clear from these verses that sanctification by the Holy Spirit is closely connected with a person's conversion and is fundamental to his entire experience of Christ. It has to do with the very beginning of God's work in a person's life. It marks the moment when the Holy Spirit makes the believer's eternal status through Christ's death an inward reality in his life.

It is easy, therefore, to see why Christians in the New Testament are so often described as 'the saints in Christ Jesus'. We can also see why Christians are spoken of as 'them which are sanctified', and in the Greek this is a perfect participle which means that a Christian's sanctification is to be regarded as an accomplished fact (see Acts 20: 32; 26: 18; 1 Cor. 1: 2).

This gives us a second possible answer to the question, 'When were you sanctified?' It is: 'I was sanctified by the Holy Spirit when He opened my eyes to the truth, convicted me of my need and brought me to the shed blood of Jesus Christ.' Incidentally this demonstrates how inappropriate it is to apply the word 'sanctification' to any experience following conversion. As Ironside summarizes these findings, 'Far from being "the second blessing", subsequent to justification, it is a work apart from which none ever would be saved.'[2]

III. SANCTIFICATION BY THE WORD OF GOD: EXTERNAL RESULTS

Clearly, we have not finished with the word 'sanctification' yet, because the Holy Spirit's work in us goes beyond setting us apart for the service of God and bringing us into a relationship with Jesus Christ. His intention is to mould our lives to the likeness of Christ Himself. So in 1 Peter 1 those who have already been addressed as 'chosen . . . and sanctified by the Spirit' are enjoined to be holy. Here is how Peter puts it: 'But

[1] R. Haldane, *The Epistle to the Romans* (Banner of Truth, 1959), p. 620.
[2] H. A. Ironside, *Holiness: the False and the True* (Pickering and Inglis, 1935), p. 57.

as he who called you is holy, be holy yourselves in all your conduct; since it is written, "You shall be holy, for I am holy" ' (1 Pet. 1: 15, 16). In other words, our eternal status which has been made inwardly real by the Holy Spirit of God now has to be worked out in terms of everyday living—'in all your conduct'. Paul was saying much the same when he called on the Philippians, 'Work out your own salvation with fear and trembling; for God is at work in you, both to will and to work for his good pleasure' (Phil. 2: 12, 13). Or, to put it more briefly, 'Work out what God has worked in'. And it is because God is working in their hearts by His Holy Spirit that Paul can expect them to go on living the Christian life even in his absence.

How, then, do we put it to practical effect? Do we just leave it passively to the Holy Spirit, and find ourselves doing naturally what we ought? Is it simply a matter of 'Love, and do as you wish'? Augustine's words are only partially true when we apply them to the matter of practical sanctification. In His Word, God has given us a pattern for Christian living. No Christian who wants to avoid sin and live a life of practical holiness can afford to ignore it. So we have the question which the psalmist both asks and answers (Ps. 119: 9), 'How can a young man keep his way pure? By guarding it according to thy word.' If the Word of God is to have the effect intended, it must be diligently obeyed. It is because there is no simple short cut to holiness that we need the sort of practical teaching which we find in the Epistles.

The third agent of sanctification, then, is the Word of God, which teaches us not only about the blood of Christ and the inward working of the Holy Spirit, but also about how God expects His provision to work out in practice. As Berkhof sees it: 'Scripture presents all the objective conditions for holy exercises and acts. It serves to excite spiritual activity by presenting motives and inducements, and gives direction to it by prohibitions, exhortations, and examples, I Pet. 1: 22; 2: 2; II Pet. 1: 4.'[1] Christ Himself recognizes the part played by the

[1] L. Berkhof, *Systematic Theology* (Banner of Truth, 1959), p. 535.

Word of God in our sanctification when He prays for His disciples, 'Sanctify them in the truth; thy word is truth' (Jn. 17: 17). This includes cleansing from sin. Jesus had already drawn attention to the cleansing effect of His Word an hour or two previously when He had been with His disciples in the upper room, 'You are already made clean by the word which I have spoken to you' (Jn. 15: 3). But here again we must remind ourselves that holiness is no mere negative concept simply involving avoidance of sin. This applies no less to its practical outworking, for a holy life is one which is unreservedly devoted to the service of God. The Word of God is an essential provision for this life. It is by the Scriptures 'that the man of God may be complete, equipped for every good work' (2 Tim. 3: 17). C. K. Barrett understands the words of our Lord's high-priestly prayer quoted above in just this positive sense. He says that the truth which is God's Word 'designates and separates the apostles for their mission'.[1]

It is important, too, to stress that the Scriptures should have an effect on the inner life of the believer. Here is one of the striking features of the new covenant which Jeremiah foresaw: 'This is the covenant which I will make with the house of Israel after those days, says the Lord: I will put my law within them, and I will write it upon their hearts' (Je. 31: 33). Paul speaks in these terms when he is writing to the Corinthians. He describes his readers as 'a letter from Christ delivered by us, written not with ink but with the Spirit of the living God, not in tablets of stone but on tablets of human hearts' (2 Cor. 3: 3). Not only does the apostle see the Word he has been ministering written in the very hearts of the Corinthians, but the Holy Spirit is the ink with which he has been writing. As a result, the Corinthians have become letters of commendation for his ministry. This was also anticipated by the writer of Psalm 119 when he declared: 'I have laid up thy word in my heart, that I might not sin against thee' (Ps. 119: 11). We have to recognize that our mind (or 'conscience' as we call it when it is dealing with moral issues) is not suffi-

[1] C. K. Barrett, *The Gospel According to St. John* (SPCK, 1956), p. 426.

cient of itself to guide us. Professor Hallesby has likened the conscience to a court of law. The latter has judicial but not legislative authority. It is not for a court to make laws or to express any opinions about existing laws, but to apply them to the situation in hand. So it is for a Christian. His conscience is not at liberty to decide general principles of right and wrong, but to apply them in given situations. Clearly, then, the conscience is only to be relied upon if it is under the law of God.

We ought not to lose sight of the importance of God's law in the matter of our sanctification, especially as many today deprecate it as the basis of Christian morality. Admittedly, the law by itself is insufficient to secure a life of practical holiness. Indeed, no part of God's Word is of any effect apart from the Holy Spirit, and this is clearly recognized in Scripture. However, we are thinking here of the person who has been set apart in his heart by the Holy Spirit and who is willing to live in fellowship with the Spirit. And it is possible for such a person to fulfil God's law. Here is how Paul puts it: 'In order that the just requirement of the law might be fulfilled in us, who walk not according to the flesh but according to the Spirit' (Rom. 8: 4). We shall return to this in chapter XIII. For the moment let us unite God's law with His Spirit, and recognize that it is the Holy Spirit's purpose to produce in the life of a Christian all that the law demands.

It would, however, be a mistake to imagine that the part God's Word plays in our sanctification is limited to issuing commands. There are also many promises in God's Word that we are encouraged to claim. William Cowper has appreciated both aspects of God's Word in these lines from a well-known hymn:

> 'Precepts and promises afford
>   A sanctifying light.'

Paul himself uses the promises of God as an incentive to practical sanctification in 2 Corinthians 7: 1: 'Since we have these promises, beloved, let us cleanse ourselves from every defilement of the body and spirit, and make holiness perfect in the fear of God.' The specific promises referred to in this case are the privileges of God's people in having Him as their Father. On this ground Christians are called upon to live a separated life, forsaking anything which would tarnish or mar their testimony.

This brings us to a third answer to our question: 'When were you sanctified?' In addition to pointing to the death of Christ on the cross and the moment when we ourselves were brought to a knowledge of Him, we can say that we are being sanctified day by day as we apply the teachings of God's Word to our lives. The practical conclusion is obvious. If anyone would live a life of holiness the study of the Bible is indispensable. It means that we read it with both a short-term and a long-term policy. Our immediate aim will be to obey it promptly, for we are to be 'doers of the word, and not hearers only' (Jas. 1: 22). At the same time our aim will also be a long-term one, for the man or woman in whom the Holy Spirit truly dwells and whose mind is constantly being filled with the Word of God is bound to find his whole outlook and attitude towards life gradually being changed, until with Luther he can say, 'My conscience is captive to the Word of God.'

CHAPTER VI

PROGRESSIVE SANCTIFICATION—RENEWAL

I T will be apparent from the last part of the previous chapter that the outworking of our sanctification is progressive. The Shorter Catechism in defining sanctification uses the word 'renewal': 'Sanctification is the work of God's free grace, whereby we are renewed in the whole man after the image of God, and are enabled more and more to die unto sin, and live unto righteousness.' In this chapter we shall examine the use and meaning of this word in Scripture. The Greek word itself means 'making new again', that is, restoring something to what was originally intended before it aged or became spoilt. This is what God does when He sanctifies a life which has been marred by sin. There is, however, another doctrine which ought to be considered first, so that we see the idea of renewal in its right context.

RENEWAL BEGINS WITH REGENERATION

We have already seen that sanctification has to do with the subjective injury which sin has done to the lives of men—with corruption and pollution. We have to bear in mind that this involves spiritual death. Men, by nature, are 'dead through . . . trespasses and sins' (Eph. 2: 1), and their minds have been blinded by the 'god of this world' (see 2 Cor. 4: 4). In short, we all need to be renewed. Now the initial stage of this is regeneration or new birth. This is fundamental to the whole process of renewal. Jesus told Nicodemus: 'Unless one is born anew, he cannot see the kingdom of God' (Jn. 3: 3). When, however, God has made him alive (Eph. 2: 5; Jn. 5: 21) and shone the light of truth into his heart (2 Cor. 4: 6) then the work of renewal has begun.

Titus 3: 5 implies that the renewing work of the Holy

Spirit follows on as a direct consequence of regeneration: 'He saved us, not because of deeds done by us in righteousness, but in virtue of his own mercy, by the washing of regeneration and renewal in the Holy Spirit.'[1] This truth is well expressed in the Prayer Book Collect for Christmas Day: 'Grant that we being regenerate . . . may daily be renewed by Thy Holy Spirit.' This, in other words, is a prayer for renewal based on the assumption of regeneration. Renewal cannot begin until a person has been born again of God's Spirit.

SOME FACTS ABOUT RENEWAL

The following references will serve as a basis for some further observations:

> 'the washing of regeneration and renewal in the Holy Spirit' (Tit. 3: 5).

> 'Do not be conformed to this world but be transformed by the renewal of your mind' (Rom. 12: 2).

> 'Though our outer nature is wasting away, our inner nature is being renewed every day' (2 Cor. 4: 16).

> You 'have put on the new nature, which is being renewed in knowledge after the image of its creator' (Col. 3: 10).

> 'Be renewed in the spirit of your minds' (Eph. 4: 23).

a. Renewal is a work of the Holy Spirit
The first of the above verses makes this clear. In other words, it is not anything we do by our own effort. This is in keeping

---

[1] It is true that, grammatically, the 'renewal in the Holy Spirit' could be taken as synonymous with 'the washing of regeneration'. D. Guthrie faces these two possibilities of interpretation and we agree with his conclusions for the reasons he gives: 'The "regeneration" and the "renewing" may be regarded as distinct operations, or both may be dependent on "washing" and therefore would describe different aspects of one operation. But since regeneration must always precede the process of renewal and since renewal is never described elsewhere as a washing, the former interpretation is to be preferred' (D. Guthrie, *The Pastoral Epistles* (Tyndale New Testament Commentary, 1957), p. 206).

with the constant teaching of the Bible. It is the Holy Spirit's work to subdue the desires of the flesh (Gal. 5: 16 ff.), to promote holiness and so on. Christian virtues are referred to as 'the fruit of the Spirit' (Gal. 5: 22 f., and cf. Eph. 5: 9). We 'worship God in the spirit' (Phil. 3: 3, AV). We love the brethren 'in the Spirit' (Col. 1: 8), and we purify our souls 'in obeying the truth through the Spirit' (1 Pet. 1: 22, AV). Lying behind every exertion of the Christian to work out his salvation is the Holy Spirit's work 'to will and to work for his good pleasure' (Phil. 2: 13). 'To will' points to the Spirit's work in creating in us the desire and intention to work out our salvation. 'To work' speaks of his work in enabling us to put this desire into effect—or to translate the Greek work literally, 'energizing' it.

b. Renewal is an inward work

It is the mind or the inward man that needs to be renewed. There is a great deal of emphasis on this in Holy Scripture. It was, for example, one of the basic needs of the children of Israel in the wilderness: 'Oh that they had such a mind as this always, to fear me and to keep all my commandments' (Dt. 5: 29). It was surely this inward work of the Holy Spirit which was foretold through the prophet Ezekiel when God said, 'And I will give them one heart, and put a new spirit within them; I will take the stony heart out of their flesh and give them a heart of flesh' (Ezk. 11: 19). That is, in place of inward deadness God intended to give life. So, then, renewal is not just a matter of copying an outward pattern, although it may well include that, but is something far deeper. 'Let this mind be in you, which was also in Christ Jesus' (Phil. 2: 5, AV) is what Paul urges upon his readers, and for a God who 'desirest truth in the inward being' (Ps. 51: 6) nothing less than this will do.

This also reminds us that sanctification involves far more than keeping a sinful nature in check, so that we live a 'life of constant victory'. It certainly includes outward victory and counteracting the insinuations of our fallen nature, but it is far more. It is a work affecting 'spirit and soul and body' (1 Thes. 5: 23). This excludes the notion of a sinful nature that remains unchanged throughout life. We may well pray:

> 'O Thou Spirit divine
> *All my nature* refine,
> Till the beauty of Jesus
> Be seen in me.'

Here is a further addition to the list of differences between sanctification and moral reformation. To show social graces and be nicely mannered is no necessary proof of inward renewal. To use the simile of Charles Hodge, 'The two things differ in nature as much as a clean heart from clean clothes.' Hodge goes on to show, in consequence, that sanctification is not to be confused with moral training: 'Such training is not to be undervalued. It is enjoined in the Word of God. It cannot, however, change the nature. It cannot impart life. A faultless statue fashioned out of pure marble in all its beauty, is far below a living man.'[1]

c. Renewal is a process

The quotations from both Corinthians and Colossians have a present passive to express the work of renewal, and this implies that it is a present process, that the inward man 'is being renewed'. At this point it is worth quoting a well-known verse where the cognate adjective, *kainos*, is employed: 'If any one is in Christ, he is a new creation; the old has passed away, behold, the new has come' (2 Cor. 5: 17; *cf.* Gal. 6: 15). A Christian, we are told here, is 'a new creation', but from what we have seen it is clear that this creation is by no means complete. It is therefore appropriate to pray in the words of Charles Wesley's well-known hymn:

> 'Finish then Thy new creation:
> Pure and spotless let us be.'

---

[1] C. Hodge, *Systematic Theology*, III (James Clarke, 1960), p. 214.

A very thrilling aspect of this process is brought out by Paul when he contrasts it with what is happening in the body: 'Though our outer nature is wasting away, our inner nature is being renewed every day' (2 Cor. 4: 16). This spiritual process, then, is a complete reversal of its bodily counterpart. The story of our bodies begins with the health and vigour of youth, and from this beginning our bodies decline to the weakness of old age and ultimately to death. Our spiritual history on the other hand is the complete opposite. Instead of having a healthy and vigorous nature, a Christian begins with a nature which is corrupted and weakened by sin. From this unpromising start the believer is daily renewed by the Holy Spirit, and can look forward to the day when this sanctifying process will be complete and he will be purged from every trace of sin. It is because of the certainty of this, the Spirit's work, that the apostle is able to say 'we do not lose heart' (2 Cor. 4: 16).

d.   Renewal requires active obedience

Although renewal is a work of the Holy Spirit, the subject is always active rather than in a state of passive surrender. He is to 'work out' his salvation. This is clear from expressions such as 'Put on the new nature', showing that the life of renewal involves a man in active obedience to God's will.

In Ephesians 4: 23 renewal is commanded. Colossians 3: 10, on the other hand, looks back to the first step in this life of obedience. Indeed, both these verses stress God's part and ours in the work of renewal. The apostle makes it quite clear that the 'new man' is not created or produced by man himself but rather 'created after the likeness of God in true righteousness and holiness' (Eph. 4: 24). The same point is made in slightly different words in the parallel reference in the Epistle to the Colossians, where Paul speaks of the 'new nature, which is being renewed in knowledge after the image of its creator' (Col. 3: 10). Nevertheless, although this new nature is created and renewed by God, Paul insists that it has to be 'put on', just as the old life has to be 'put off'.

From the Scriptures we have quoted it will be apparent that man's part in his sanctification is not independent of the Holy Spirit. We are not to imagine that sanctification is partly God's work and partly ours. There is no division of labour, as if God said, 'You do your part and I will do Mine.' Rather, our moral exertions and the diligence with which we use the means of grace are the instruments by which God effects our sanctification.

So the call to sanctification is often issued as a command. Where the Spirit of God is renewing a person He challenges him to action. Take, for example, the call to the people of Isaiah's day to cleanse themselves deliberately from all sinful and doubtful things, and positively to devote themselves to good works: 'Wash yourselves; make yourselves clean; remove the evil of your doings from before my eyes; cease to do evil; learn to do good; seek justice, correct oppression; defend the fatherless, plead for the widow' (Is. 1: 16, 17). Jeremiah makes a similar command: 'O Jerusalem, wash your heart from wickedness' (Je. 4: 14). Then again, the verse in 2 Corinthians quoted earlier: 'Since we have these promises . . . let us cleanse ourselves from every defilement of body and spirit' (2 Cor. 7: 1). The way to cleanse our conduct is 'by *guarding it* according to thy word' (Ps. 119: 9). This will certainly involve us in a fight against the devil's temptations, and we shall need to remember James' word: 'Resist the devil and he will flee from you' (Jas. 4: 7). To summarize, in the words of John Owen: 'God works in us and with us, not against us or without us; so that His assistance is an encouragement as to the facilitating of the work, and no occasion of neglect as to the work itself.'[1]

This, of course, is one of the ways in which the process of renewal differs from regeneration. In regeneration we are passive. We can no more help ourselves than a baby can help in its own birth. But in our renewal, far from being passive, we are fellow-workers with God.

[1] J. Owen, *Temptation and Sin* (Zondervan, 1959), p. 20.

c. Renewal works to a pattern

The ultimate goal of renewal is 'the image of him that created him'. It is the very nature and character of God Himself towards which the Christian is growing. By his regeneration he has been born into God's family, and as he grows up he is to show more and more of the family likeness. This will entail growing into the likeness of God's holiness. In this context Christ can be regarded as the elder brother in the family of God. He is the perfect example of how the character of God Himself can be expressed in human life. So instead of being 'conformed to this world', a Christian is 'to be conformed to the image of his Son, in order that he might be the firstborn among many brethren' (Rom. 8: 29).

CHAPTER VII

SANCTIFICATION AND JUSTIFICATION

W E now come to the all-important matter of distinguishing sanctification and justification. We have already seen in chapter IV that these two doctrines correspond to the two main effects of sin. Justification deals with man's condemnation in God's sight, while sanctification is the answer to his sinful condition. Having studied the biblical usage of 'sanctify' and 'renew', we are now in a position to pursue further the differences and relationship between these two doctrines. We will begin with a brief summary of the doctrine of justification, and then go on to see where sanctification differs from it.

THE MEANING OF JUSTIFICATION

The word 'justification' is basically a legal term. This is already apparent from our introduction to it at the end of chapter IV. It will become still more apparent from the following quotation, which is fairly typical of the use of this word in Scripture: 'If there is a dispute between men, and they come into court, and the judges decide between them, acquitting' (AV, 'justify') 'the innocent and condemning the wicked . . .' (Dt. 25: 1). From this verse it is clear that justifying a man does not affect his moral condition. When a judge declares a man 'Not Guilty', he is simply giving him a legal standing. The same applies in legal practice today. When a jury give a verdict of 'Not Guilty', they are not reforming the prisoner, nor are they making any moral difference to him. Rather, on the basis of the evidence which they have been considering, they declare that, in the eyes of the law, the man is to be treated as 'Not Guilty', and as a result the judge acquits him. Deuteronomy 25: 1 also clearly shows that 'justify' is the opposite of 'condemn'. This is also plain from Jesus' statement: 'By your words you will be justified, and by your words you will be condemned' (Mt. 12: 37).

What happens to a sinner when he stands before God, who is 'the Judge of all the earth' (Gn. 18: 25)? The Bible has only one answer: he is condemned. Judged by the standards of God's law, he has come hopelessly short. He has broken 'the great and first commandment' (Mt. 22: 38) simply by failing to give God the place in his life which is His due. Of course, most of us at some time try to excuse ourselves and pretend that we are quite good enough because we manage to appear sufficiently respectable before the eyes of our fellow human beings. All this, however, is unavailing before God. He has before Him all the evidence, including the true condition of our hearts. Jesus pointed that out to the Pharisees, 'You are those who justify yourselves before men, but God knows your hearts' (Lk. 16: 15). If we face the true facts of God's law, we are surely forced to confess with the psalmist, 'Enter not into judgment with thy servant; for no man living is righteous before thee' (Ps. 143: 2).

How then can a sinner be justified (declared righteous) by a holy and righteous God? How is he to attain the legal standing of 'Not Guilty' in the sight of such a judge? In human law there is only one way for a guilty man to be justified, and that is by the sentence which the law requires being carried out. Once this has been completed and the law's requirements have been satisfied, then, as far as the law is concerned, he is free of his guilt. But this is no answer to the problem of a sinner found guilty before God, for 'the wages of sin is death' (Rom. 6: 23), physical and spiritual, eternal and final.

Yet God in His grace and mercy has made it possible for sinners to be declared righteous before Him. This is how the apostle Paul expresses it: 'They are justified by his grace as a gift, through the redemption which is in Christ Jesus, whom God put forward as an expiation' (AV, 'propitiation') 'by his blood, to be received by faith. This was to show God's righteousness, because in his divine forbearance he had passed over former sins' (Rom. 3: 24, 25).

This means that when Christ shed His blood on the cross, He died the death which was our due, in our place and on our behalf, and, as the apostle Paul continues: 'it was to prove at the present time that he himself is righteous and that he justifies him who has faith in Jesus' (Rom. 3: 26). As a result, 'There is therefore now no condemnation for those who are in Christ Jesus' (Rom. 8: 1), and so, on the ground of what Jesus Christ has done on the cross, God can pronounce the sinner who believes in Christ, 'Not Guilty', 'Uncondemned', 'Justified'.

WHERE SANCTIFICATION DIFFERS

If this brief description of justification is now compared with the biblical teaching on sanctification, striking differences clearly emerge. The former is legal, external and objective, whereas sanctification, which is to do with the purifying of the heart and life, is experimental, internal and subjective. Instead of being concerned with our outward standing, sanctification applies to our inward condition. And there is another difference. A man is justified by a sovereign, once-for-all declaration of God the Father, just as a court of law makes a similar declaration concerning the defendant. Sanctification, on the other hand, is a gradual process which is effected by the inner working of the Holy Spirit of God. The process begins when the Holy Spirit first sets a sinner apart and gives him new life by the act of regeneration. It continues in the inward renewal of his nature. It is not completed until the end of this present life, when he is glorified and made like Christ. We shall consider this final stage of sanctification, usually called 'glorification', in chapter XIV.[1]

Failure to distinguish between justification and sanctifi-

---

[1] As we saw in chapter V, sanctification, both in the Epistle to the Hebrews and in the writings of Paul, *includes* an aspect which is positional, objective and external. For this reason we must recognize that the use of the word 'sanctify' in the Epistle to the Hebrews brings it very close in meaning to justification. This does not mean, however,

cation is one of the errors of the Roman Catholic church. It is assumed that justification has to do with being *made* (as distinct from being *declared*) righteous. No doubt the Latin language has helped to create this confusion, for *justificio*, from which the English 'justify' is derived, was an unfortunate way to translate the Hebrew and Greek word we have been studying. This Latin word does in fact mean literally, 'to make righteous', which, as we have seen, is not the meaning of the Hebrew and Greek of Scripture. The Roman Catholic church has made many attempts to discover its doctrine in Scripture. In a fairly recent textbook of Roman Catholic teaching, Ludwig Ott claims that justification is 'a true eradication of sin' and further explains: 'Holy Writ conceives the forgiveness of sins as a real and complete removal of the sins.'[1] This is tantamount to saying that it is sanctification. He then attempts to uphold this statement with a list of Bible expressions, complete with biblical references, but it is noticeable that the word 'justify' is strangely missing from all his examples! For his statement that 'Scripture represents justification . . . as a sanctification', he quotes 1 Corinthians 6: 11!

The different modes of appropriation

One of the very important differences between these two doctrines is the response which they demand from man. Notice first of all, however, that both 'justification' and 'sanctification' are secured by faith. 'Justification by faith' is one of the

that in Hebrews the word can simply be included under the heading of justification. The latter is the language of the law courts and has to do with our legal standing, but 'sanctify' is from the language of Old Testament worship and relates to purity. Also we have to remember that Paul, too, speaks of positional sanctification in, for example, his reference to all Christians as 'saints', irrespective of their progress in practical sanctification. This does not mean that for him it was just a synonym for justification!

The important point seems to be this. Although sanctification is essentially inward, progressive and experimental, it is based on the objective work of Christ just as much as justification. So Christ is 'made our . . . righteousness' (*i.e.*, justification) 'and sanctification . . .' (1 Cor. 1: 30).

[1] L. Ott, *Fundamentals of Catholic Dogma* (Mercier Press, 1955), p. 250.

cardinal doctrines in Scripture, and it is when a man believes in Christ that God declares him righteous. This is especially emphasized in the Epistle to the Romans.[1] Faith is also essential to sanctification, and in Acts we have that very expression, 'sanctified by faith' (26: 18). So when the apostle told the Philippian jailer, 'Believe in the Lord Jesus, and you will be saved' (Acts 16: 31), there is every reason to believe that Paul had in mind salvation in all its aspects, including sanctification.

They differ, however, over the place given to works and effort. In justification these have no place at all. This was what Luther meant by *per fidem solam*, 'by faith alone'. There is nothing that we can do to earn or merit our justification, for no matter how hard we try we still fall short of the moral standards that God has revealed in His law. Paul emphasizes this when he says, 'For by grace you have been saved through faith; and this is not your own doing, it is the gift of God—not because of works, lest any man should boast' (Eph. 2: 8, 9). Paul is surely thinking here of the Christian's justification which is a past, accomplished fact, rather than his sanctification, which is essentially a present process. This is apparent from his use of the perfect participle which could be fairly translated, 'By grace are you *in a position of having been saved through faith.*'

This is a further point of difference with the Roman Catholic church. Canon 24 of the Council of Trent states: 'If anyone saith, that the justice received is not preserved and also increased before God through good works; but that the said works are merely the fruits and signs of Justification obtained, but not a cause of the increase thereof; let him be anathema.' Notice that not only do good works play a part in justification according to the Roman Catholic church, but justification itself is a matter of degree and can be increased. Here again is a basic defection from the teaching of Holy Scripture. Furthermore, it is perhaps significant that the chapter on Justification in Ludwig Ott's work, from which we have already quoted, is headed 'The Process of Justification'. However, since this

[1] See 3: 24–31 and the example of Abraham in chapter 4.

confusion in Roman teaching does more damage to the doctrine of justification than sanctification, we will say no more about it here.

Whereas we are justified 'through faith alone' our sanctification involves both faith and effort. In the verse following our Ephesians quotation Paul goes on to speak of sanctification. Salvation is 'not . . . of works' but it is 'for good works', and surely the very word 'work' implies effort. So when we are thinking of our justification it is certainly true to insist 'It is no good trying to be good'. But when the Holy Spirit is sanctifying the sinner, it is all part of the process to challenge and stimulate him to work and effort. As we saw in our last chapter, the work of renewal requires of the sinner, not passive surrender, but active obedience. This will become even more apparent in chapter XI, when we shall see that sanctification requires considerable effort and discipline on the part of the believer.

The following table may help us to appreciate the difference between these two doctrines:

JUSTIFICATION	SANCTIFICATION
1. Concerns guilt	Concerns pollution
2. Legal, external, objective	Experimental, internal, subjective
3. Relates to our standing	Relates to our condition
4. Righteousness imputed	Righteousness imparted
5. Has no degrees (*i.e.*, a person is either 'Guilty' or 'Not Guilty'. No-one is described as 'Slightly Guilty' or 'Fairly Guilty')	Has degrees (some are worse offenders than others)
6. Once-for-all and not repeated	A gradual process
7. By declaration of God the Father	By operation of the Holy Spirit
8. Our works have no place	Man co-operates by moral exertion and personal discipline

THE CONNECTION BETWEEN JUSTIFICATION AND SANCTIFICATION

Although these two doctrines must be carefully distinguished, they are never separated in experience. We cannot have one without the other. Every sinner needs both, for sin never condemns a person without also defiling him. At the same time, God meets both needs, for when He saves a man He does it completely. However, many have misunderstood the inseparable nature of these two aspects of salvation, and so we emphasize the connection from either side.

a. No sanctification without justification

To suppose that a man must become righteous before he can be declared righteous is a mistake of the natural man. Human wisdom teaches it. God has revealed that it is the other way about. Indeed, until a person is justified he is under God's condemnation, and so is in no position to be sanctified, for he is cut off from the only One who can do it. This is how the New Testament frequently describes the position of Christians before they believed in Christ, as 'alienated . . . and strangers . . . having no hope and without God' (Eph. 2: 12). So until a man believes in Christ he is quite unable to please God, for 'whatever does not proceed from faith is sin' (Rom. 14: 23).

This is the important truth which is stressed in Article 13 of the Church of England, 'Of works before justification'. Here is how it is expressed: 'Works done before the grace of Christ, and the inspiration of His Spirit, are not pleasant to God, forasmuch as they spring not of faith in Jesus Christ, neither do they make men meet to receive grace . . . yea rather, for that they are not done as God hath willed and commanded them to be done, we doubt not but they have the nature of sin.'

b. No justification without sanctification

Some well-meaning Christians speak of being justified on one date and then sanctified subsequently. Others talk about accepting Jesus as Saviour and later receiving Him as Lord. Yet another variation on the same theme is to speak of an experience of the Holy Spirit as something quite separate and distinct from the benefits of Christ's death on the cross. Most of the forms of perfectionism we shall consider in chapter VIII are based upon this separation. Here is yet another way in which the doctrine of sanctification is misunderstood, sometimes expressed as: 'You received your justification by a simple act of faith without any effort on your part. In the same way you can be sanctified, by receiving it as a gift by simple faith.'

It is important to notice that justification and sanctification are kept together in Scripture. Paul writes: 'He is the source of your life in Christ Jesus, whom God made our wisdom, our righteousness' (*i.e.*, justification) 'and sanctification and redemption' (1 Cor. 1: 30). Those who are 'in Christ Jesus', then, have Him in all these aspects. Even though there was so much moral failure in the lives of the Corinthian Christians that Paul had to describe them as carnal and not spiritual, they are still addressed as 'saints', and Paul writes concerning them: 'But you were washed, you were sanctified, you were justified in the name of the Lord Jesus Christ and in the Spirit of our God' (1 Cor. 6: 11). Such is the very purpose of God in choosing us to be His people: 'Whom he foreknew he also predestined to be conformed to the image of his Son . . .' (Rom. 8: 29). 'He chose us in him before the foundation of the world, that we should be holy and blameless before him' (Eph. 1: 4). To look at it another way, good works are an essential result of living faith. If faith produces no good works it can be no more than barren orthodoxy (see Jas. 2: 17–20).

This last quotation touches on another important point. Sanctification is a necessary result of justification, and to imagine that a man can be justified without any change for the better in his moral condition reveals a defective view of both doctrines. So Warfield: 'Sanctification is but the execution of the justifying decree. For it to fail would be for the acquitted person not to be released in accordance with his acquittal.'[1]

The attempt to separate justification and sanctification by a lapse of time also points to a defective view of faith in Christ.

[1] B. B. Warfield, *Perfectionism* (PRPC, 1958), p. 100.

On what scriptural ground can it be asserted that you can believe for justification one day and on a later occasion believe for sanctification? Nowhere in the Bible is faith divided up like that. If justification necessarily leads to sanctification then justifying faith is identical with sanctifying faith, and that faith is faith in Christ, who is both our justification and our sanctification, rather than faith in any doctrine. We cannot fragment salvation into numerous distinct particles, each of which is to be sought and acquired by a separate act of faith. This is not just a matter of fussing over doctrinal exactness, for the error we are considering has more sinister implications. To imagine that a person can be justified without also being sanctified is very close to the suggestion that Paul rejects so completely at the beginning of Romans 6. Indeed, the objection which Paul anticipates in the opening verse in the words: 'Are we to continue in sin that grace may abound?', could well be re-written: 'Are we to neglect sanctification because of the benefits of justification?'

T. C. Hammond brings out the gravity of this implication when he writes: 'Its great danger is to suggest that the work of God in justification is, if we may so express it, a bare minimum which secures salvation but does not seriously affect the life. We find such statements made as that Jesus is taken as Saviour but is not acknowledged as Lord. If this is only a loose and unguarded way of saying that many Christians live far below the great possibilities opened for them in the life of full surrender it would not be necessary to do more than point out that it is an unguarded way of speaking. But when the idea is extended to suggest that it is possible to continue in a low state of Christian living in full consciousness that there are other demands pressed upon us by God which we can afford to ignore if we merely wish to escape condemnation, and are indifferent to any crown of reward, then indeed it becomes a most serious evil and may lead people to nourish an utterly false hope'[1]

[1] T. C. Hammond, *The New Creation* (Marshall, Morgan and Scott, 1953), p. 151.

CHAPTER VIII

PERFECTIONISM

PERFECTIONISM is an error which is always appearing in one form or another. What it states, simply, is that it is possible for a Christian to live sinlessly, to be perfect in the sense that he fulfils all that God requires of him. This error was certainly known in the days of the early church, and may well have been in Paul's mind as he wrote Philippians 3. Various forms of the teaching have also been held by the Roman Catholic church. All modern perfectionist movements, however, seem to stem from the views of John Wesley, at least in some modified form, for it was Wesley who first gave the idea prominence in Protestant circles. It has been hailed by some as Wesley's distinctive contribution to the church, and has even been compared with Luther's rediscovery of the doctrine of justification by faith. Wesley himself never claimed to have attained to perfection. Indeed, in a letter published in a London journal when he was sixty-four, he distinctly denied that he himself had ever experienced it. Many of his successors have not shown the same reticence!

Wesley expressed his view in the doctrine of 'Perfect Love', based on the reference to this expression in 1 John 4. We will not attempt to explain Wesley's exposition of this passage. Bishop Stephen Neill has said enough to discourage us from that! 'Even the best expositors have difficulty in making plain, to themselves and to others, exactly what Wesley meant by his doctrine of "perfect love".'[1] In any case, before we come to consider what the Bible teaches on this subject and to discuss the scriptures claimed in its support, we ought to be aware of a basic presupposition underlying almost all perfectionist teaching.

This is the assumption that obligation is determined by

[1] S. C. Neill, *Christian Holiness* (Lutterworth, 1960), p. 31.

ability. It was first propounded by Pelagius, a British monk who lived in the fourth and fifth centuries, and who has given his name to the view of sin and grace known as Pelagianism. His fundamental proposition was this: because God has commanded man to do what is good he must have the ability to do it, and so man has a will which is absolutely free. In order to assert this, Pelagius found it necessary to deny any idea of a sinful nature in man. Sin, he taught, consists only in separate acts of the will. For Pelagius this meant that perfection is a possibility for the unaided, natural man. He can do all that God requires of him.

Some perfectionists have followed Pelagius both in his presupposition that obligation is determined by ability, and in the deductions he makes from it about the moral ability of the natural man. C. G. Finney, for example, a perfectionist of the nineteenth century, adapted his understanding of God's law to this presupposition, and even claimed to find justification for his theory in the language of the 'first and great commandment': 'The very language of the law is such as to level its claims to the capacity of the subject however great or small that subject may be. "Thou shalt love the Lord thy God with all thy heart, with all thy soul, with all thy mind, and with all thy strength." Here then it is plain, that all the law demands, is the exercise of whatever strength we have, in the service of God. Now as entire sanctification consists in perfect obedience to the law of God, and as the law requires nothing more than the right use of whatever strength we have, it is, of course, forever settled, that a state of entire sanctification is attainable in this life, *on the ground of natural ability*.'[1] Professor G. Walters, to whom I am indebted for this quotation, comments: 'This is based on a lamentable misunderstanding of Dt. vi. 5.'[2] Who can be blamed for regarding Finney as a Pelagian? However, by no means all forms of perfectionism would go as far as this. Most would apply the basic Pelagian principle only to the regenerate, to the Christian who is a

[1] C. G. Finney, *Systematic Theology* (1851), p. 407; italics mine.
[2] G. Walters, *The New Bible Dictionary* (IVF, 1962), p. 1141.

partaker of God's grace. God demands from His redeemed people perfection. So, it is argued, such perfection must be possible to a Christian because God would not demand from him anything of which he is incapable. Some put it like this. Attention is drawn first of all to the low standard of living of many Christians, and it has of course been possible to do this in every age. 'Is this God's purpose?' it is asked. If not, then some higher life must be possible. An attempt must then be made to define what is possible, and if this does not include the eradication of the sinful nature, then perhaps it includes the possibility of keeping that nature under control and living a life of constant victory. If sanctification is a matter of growth then perhaps at every stage in our development there is a limited degree of growth that God requires, and such a degree is possible to us. But notice the same assumption running through all the forms this doctrine takes: what is demanded of us must be possible.

Yet this proposition does not seem to occur in Scripture, which nowhere equates obligation with ability. Look, for example, at John 8, where in the one passage we find Jesus telling His hearers that they were the bond-slaves of sin and unable to hear His word, and yet at the same time that they would die in their sin. So, even though they were slaves of sin, God would still hold them accountable. Paul teaches precisely the same thing. Men are under obligation to God's law, yet they are unable to fulfil its demands.

The absurdity of the Pelagian principle can be seen when it is applied in other directions, as B. B. Warfield demonstrates. First of all, he quotes from Finney an example of the type of argument we have been considering: ' "If it is not a practic-able duty to be perfectly holy in this world, then it will follow that the devil has so completely accomplished his design of corrupting mankind, that Jesus Christ is at fault, and has no way to sanctify His people but by taking them out of the world. . . . If perfect sanctification is not attainable in this world, it must be either from a want of motives in the Gospel, or a want of sufficient power in the Spirit of God." ' To this

Warfield replies: 'It would be a poor reader indeed who did not perceive at once that such dilemmas could be applied equally to every evil with which man is afflicted—disease, death, the uncompleted salvation of the world. If it is not a practicable thing to be perfectly well in this world, then Jesus Christ has been vanquished by the devil and has no way to make His people well except by taking them out of the world. If freedom from death is not attainable in this world, then it must be due to want of sufficient power in the Spirit of God. If the world does not become at once the pure Kingdom of God in which only righteousness dwells, then we must infer either a want of sufficient motives in the Gospel or a want of sufficient power in the Son of God. There have been people who reasoned thus: the point of interest now is, that it was not otherwise that Finney reasoned—and that accounts for many things besides his perfectionism. It is a simple matter of fact that the effects of redemption, in the individual and in the world at large, are realized, not all at once, but through a long process: and that their complete enjoyment lies only "at the end".'[1]

BIBLICAL CONSIDERATIONS

We now turn to the scriptural passages which are sometimes quoted in support of perfectionism. There are, for example, commands to be perfect. Our Lord said: 'You, therefore, must be perfect, as your heavenly Father is perfect' (Mt. 5: 48). We have already seen that our ability cannot be determined from the commandments of God. But what about cases where believers are described as 'perfect'? We find Paul speaking of 'them that are perfect' (1 Cor. 2: 6, AV) and 'as many as be perfect' (Phil. 3: 15, AV). Notice, however, it does not say 'sinlessly perfect'. The word can equally be well translated 'full grown' and in itself means no more than this. This is in fact how the Authorized Version translates it in Hebrew 5: 14. The Revised Standard Version employs 'mature' in all these cases, except the one in Matthew.

[1] B. B. Warfield, *Perfectionism* (PRPC, 1958), pp. 39 f.

The same applies to the passage about 'perfect love' employed by John Wesley (1 Jn. 4: 17–21). There is no need to argue, as some have done rather unconvincingly, that the apostle John is still referring to God's love for us, as he has been in the previous verses. More naturally, it is to our love for God that he now turns. But there is still little in this verse on which to base a doctrine of sinless perfection. J. R. W. Stott comments: 'John is not suggesting that any Christian's love could in this life be flawlessly perfect, but rather developed and mature, set fixedly upon God.'[1]

Two other verses in the same Epistle are often held out as proof texts for sinless perfection. They are the statements: 'No one born of God commits sin' (1 Jn. 3: 9) and 'We know that any one born of God does not sin' (1 Jn. 5: 18). At first sight perhaps they do appear to teach this, although if the method of interpretation is correct they really prove too much. They would mean that sinless perfection is not only possible for a Christian, but inevitable! This in itself should be enough to demonstrate that the perfectionist method of interpretation cannot be the right one. John is here writing of something which applies to every child of God, and it cannot mean that each one is sinless, because he makes explicit reference to the provision God has made for believers when they sin (see, *e.g.*, 1 Jn. 2: 1 f.). The most natural explanation is that John is describing here the essential nature of the new life of a Christian. The many scholars who have understood John's meaning in this way have usually drawn attention to the present tense employed in the Greek, which expresses the idea that the one who is born of God does not go on sinning continually. This, for example, is how Berkhof understands it: 'In view of the fact that John invariably uses the present to express the idea that the one born of God does not sin, it is possible that he desires to express the idea that the child of God does not go on sinning habitually, as the devil does.'[2] When giving the Bible

---

[1] J. R. W. Stott, *The Epistles of John* (Tyndale New Testament Commentary, 1964), p. 168.

[2] L. Berkhof, *Systematic Theology* (Banner of Truth, 1959), p. 539.

readings at the Keswick Convention in 1959 on this Epistle, Professor E. M. Blaiklock explained it like this: 'The verse, of course, must be read in the context of the whole letter. The present tense in the Greek verb implied habit, continuity, unbroken sequence. A Christian is quite capable of sinning. That is a sad fact of common experience, and John has recognized it and named the remedy while admitting the fact. Nevertheless, opposition to sin, and hatred of it, is the ruling principle of life. A Christian may fail and fall, but the enemy has but brief triumph. The fallen rises again, confesses his fault, and presses on. The habitual sinner does none of these things. Just as the apostates who had left the Church proved, in John's view, that they had never belonged to it, so the one who "continues in sin", who covets no change, and seeks no victory, proves in the act that he had never known Christ. The true Christian echoes Paul, "Who shall deliver me from the body of this death? I thank God through Jesus Christ our Lord." '[1]

It is sometimes said that John's words, 'The blood of Jesus his Son cleanses us from all sin' (1 Jn. 1: 7), declare the possibility of an immediate and complete deliverance from the power of sin. But this interpretation fails to take into consideration the context in which the verse is found. As Bishop Stephen Neill writes on this and the previous verse, 'So far from excluding the possibility of sinning, John is here presupposing it, and is indicating how this continuing reality in the life of the church is to be dealt with.'[2]

All this shows that the verses used to support the doctrine of sinless perfection will not bear the weight that is placed upon them. But we can go further than this to demonstrate that the doctrine is contradicted by Scripture. For one thing, there is clear evidence that the New Testament Christians were not themselves sinlessly perfect; and this includes the apostles. Paul, for example, had a sharp contention with Barnabas on one occasion, and with Peter on another. Moreover, we find

[1] E. M. Blaiklock, *The Keswick Week*, 1959, pp. 92 f.
[2] S. C. Neill, *Christian Holiness* (Lutterworth, 1960), p. 35.

some of the holiest men in the Bible confessing their sins. Indeed, there are clear statements that no-one is sinless. Solomon declared: 'There is no man who does not sin' (1 Ki. 8:46), while John maintains that those who claim to the contrary are victims of self-deception (1 Jn. 1:8). Sin is a constant problem to be faced in the Christian life; there is an unceasing conflict between the spirit and the flesh (Gal. 5:16 ff.). Is it not significant that the Lord's Prayer includes prayers for forgiveness and deliverance from temptation and the evil one? Presumably these are numbered amongst the normal needs of a Christian and so are included in the pattern prayer.

MODIFICATIONS OF PERFECTIONISM

Many who have acknowledged the untenability of absolute perfectionism, but who still cling to the Pelagian presupposition underlying it, have suggested some modifications to this doctrine. The alternative theories, all based on the assumption that obligation is determined by opportunity, are distinguished by their various assessments of the moral capability of a Christian. Their exponents search the Scriptures to see if a formula exists whereby their own particular type of perfectionism may be obtained. They often strongly contest sinless perfection, recognizing it to be well beyond man's reach in this life, without realizing that their alternative propositions really amount to the same thing in another form.

There are a number of theories, perhaps almost as many theories as there are exponents, but there are one or two features common to them all. They all understand sanctification to be an isolated experience subsequent to justification. Just as justification is received from God by an act of faith, so is sanctification received by another separate and specific act of faith. This interpretation is hardly in keeping with the biblical usage of these terms which we have observed in earlier chapters, so we need say no more about it now.

Another feature is the way these theories tend to externalize sin and fail to do justice to the inward corruption of human

nature which we considered in chapter IV. An example of
this is the view that present sanctification consists in keeping
the sinful nature under control and in subjection. 'Counter-
action' is the word often used to describe this. Some preachers
have been bold enough to offer believers the possibility of
living 'a life of constant victory' with the inner sinful nature
kept under control. It is difficult to distinguish this view from
perfectionism except that it is limited to eradicating external
acts of sin. Of course, there is a truth contained in it. Present
sanctification most certainly does include keeping our sinful
nature in subjection. After all, does not Paul enjoin his readers
to 'make no provision for the flesh, to gratify its desires' (Rom.
13: 14)? However, this is only part of the truth and this part
alone would give a poor conception of salvation in Christ.
This view overlooks the inward character of sin which we
faced in chapter IV, and the fact that sanctification is as much
concerned with the sinful nature as with external acts.
Renewal, as we saw in chapter VI, is an inward work, and
Paul speaks of God 'sanctifying us wholly', which includes
our whole 'spirit and soul and body' (1 Thes. 5: 23). Sanctification is a radical transformation brought about in man's
innermost being and nature. The Holy Spirit 'makes the tree
good that the fruit may be good'.[1]

Another frequent tendency of these theories is to lower the
standard of holiness. This seems to be the only way of being
able to substantiate a claim to perfection. They suggest that
God requires less of us under grace than He did under law.
Obviously this unscriptural notion could be a very dangerous
one. Indeed, history shows many examples of perfectionism
leading to a low standard of Christian living and even scan-
dalous behaviour. Bishop Handley Moule's experience is an
example: 'As far as my own observation goes, such views are
not uncommonly attended, in those who hold them, by a
certain oblivion to personal shortcomings and inconsistencies;
by an obscuration of consciousness, and of conscience, more
or less marked, towards the sinfulness of ordinary, everyday

[1] B. B. Warfield, *Perfectionism* (PRPC, 1958), p. 368.

violations of the law of holiness in respect of "meekness, humbleness of mind, longsuffering", sympathy, and other quiet graces.'[1] Perhaps this is not really surprising. A doctrinaire clinging to perfection, despite practical evidence to the contrary, can lead a person to assume that all he does must be right, and so, to use the oft-quoted forceful phrase of Dr. J. S. Whale, 'Belief in the inner light may be the shortest road to the outer darkness.' Or as Bishop Stephen Neill wrote: 'It might almost seem as though, under the judgment of God, the highest claims prepared the way for the deepest falls.'[2]

One particularly ingenious idea is that perfection involves freedom from conscious sinning. Again, we refer back to our chapter on sin to refute this, and again point out how important it is to have a right understanding of sin in order to have a correct view of holiness. Notice, we describe this view as 'ingenious': it is, because it provides a way of combining some form of perfection with that of Christian growth. The idea is that in this life we come short of the holiness of Christ. But we can be perfect to the best of our limited knowledge. Growth in grace involves the progressive uncovering of our unconscious sinfulness, and as this proceeds, so the blood of Christ is available for our cleansing. As Pearsall Smith, a nineteenth-century advocate of the view, explained: ' "The blood cleanseth"—is ever cleansing sin *from the conscience*, as it is progressively revealed.' B. B. Warfield, to whom we are indebted for this quotation, adds, 'which is not exactly what I John i. 7 says.'[3] Our conscience's dictates do not form the biblical standard by which our perfection is to be judged. B. B. Warfield has surely put his finger right on the weakness of the whole theory when he writes: 'The standard being a subjective, not an objective one, our knowledge, not God's law, Christian perfection does not mean the fulfilling of all that God requires of a Christian, but only of all that a Chris-

[1] H. C. G. Moule, *Philippian Studies* (Pickering and Inglis, 1956), p. 188.
[2] S. C. Neill, *Christian Holiness* (Lutterworth, 1960), p. 37.
[3] B. B. Warfield, *Perfectionism* (PRPC, 1958), p. 279; italics his.

tian's conscience, in its changing degrees of knowledge, requires from time to time of himself. The subjectiveness of the thought is intense, and one is tempted to apply the proverb, "Where ignorance is bliss, 'tis folly to be wise".[1]

Closely connected with this view and often combined with it is another modification of perfectionism we ought to notice. It is the idea that a Christian can be perfect at every stage of his development. What he is growing towards is not perfection, because he has this already, but rather maturity. The Christian has often been likened to a growing baby or a maturing apple, as the following extract shows:

'The little babe may be all that a babe could be, or ought to be, and may therefore perfectly please its mother; and yet it is very far from being what that mother would wish it to be when the years of maturity shall come.

'The apple in June is a perfect apple for June; it is the best apple that June can produce: but it is very different from the apple in October, which is a perfected apple.'[2]

Here is yet another example of a completely inadequate view of sin and the corruption of human nature. Again, B. B. Warfield spots the basic error and shows the unsuitability of this analogy: 'The human "apple in June" is not merely an immature apple, it is a rotten apple. It does not merely need "to grow" in order to become the "perfected" apple of October, it has got to be remade before it becomes the perfect apple for June and is in a state to "grow" at all.'[3] To regard the Christian life as a process of growth is quite scriptural, but to view every stage of growth as perfection is quite inappropriate for a Christian whose nature is corrupt and worldly and is always in conflict with God's Spirit. Then this again raises the question of the standard by which our lives are to be judged. Bishop Stephen Neill is surely right to ask: 'Is man once again to be the measure of all things? By what standard am I to be

[1] B. B. Warfield, *Perfectionism* (PRPC, 1958), pp. 279 f.
[2] Mrs. Hannah Pearsall Smith, *The Christian's Secret of a Happy Life* (Nisbet, 1888), p. 36.
[3] B. B. Warfield, *Perfectionism* (PRPC, 1958), p. 305.

judged? Is my unaided capacity at any one moment to be the measure at that moment of Christian attainment and Christian expectation?'[1]

BIBLICAL PERFECTIONISM

Now we must be positive, because, in facing the errors of a false perfectionism, we must not lose sight of what the Bible does teach on this subject. We have seen that the word 'perfect' means 'mature'. Are we then really seeking the maturity of which the Bible speaks? Are we showing the maturity of those who are skilful in the Word of God (Heb. 5: 11 ff.)? Are we showing the stability which accompanies maturity, or are we still the children of whom Paul writes: 'tossed to and fro and carried about with every wind of doctrine' (Eph. 4: 14)?

And let us not fail to recognize that although perfectionism is an error, a much needed emphasis has often been given by many of its exponents. Perfectionist movements often arise as a protest against the low standard of Christian living and commitment. Sinless perfection may not be attainable in this life, but it is nonetheless the goal. It is not difficult to see the possible dangers in the attitude which says, 'Well, of course, we cannot be perfect, can we?' The right balance is carefully maintained in Scripture. Take the first Epistle of John, for example; one moment the writer is warning us that, 'If we say we have no sin, we deceive ourselves, and the truth is not in us.' A moment later he is urging, 'I am writing this to you so that you may not sin' (1 Jn. 1: 8 and 2: 1). Here is the attitude of heart that is to be ours. The aim of a Christian should always be 'that you may not sin'. Paul knew something of this, too; having set aside all claims to perfection he declared that nonetheless perfection was his goal. 'One thing I do', he wrote, 'forgetting those things which are behind, and reaching forth unto those things which are before, I press toward the mark for the prize of the high calling of God in Christ Jesus.' And perhaps the following verse puts Paul's statement

[1] S. C. Neill, *Christian Holiness* (Lutterworth, 1960), p. 38.

right into the context of our subject: 'Let us therefore, as many as be perfect, be thus minded' (Phil. 3: 13 ff., AV).

High aims and ideals are always important to a Christian. Bishop Stephen Neill detects a similarity between the Christian and the artist at this point: 'We can learn a religious truth from the artists. The great among them have ever striven for a perfection of expression that they knew could never be attained—and in the ever-frustrated effort have left us monuments of their greatness. Others have early attained a certain slick perfection of technique; and have made it astonishingly plain to us how banal even excellent painting can be, if uninspired by that ideal that ever flees before the questing eye and hand of the artist.'[1] John, in 1 John 2: 1, not only holds before us the ideal of sinlessness; he also gives advice towards the attainment of that ideal. This, he says, is one of the purposes in his writing: 'I am writing *this* to you so that you may not sin.' We naturally ask, 'What is *this*?' and of course in answering the question we could well study the whole Bible, to which the word 'this' clearly applies. What, however, is John pointing to in the immediate context of his Epistle? It is surely to three important facts, which he mentioned in the previous chapter. The facts are presented here in the form of three mistakes a Christian is to avoid.

First of all, a Christian should avoid having a wrong view of God (1 Jn. 1: 5, 6). The error exposed in verse 6 amounts to this, that sin does not really matter. It is based on an idea that God is very easy-going; 'God is light and in him is no darkness at all' is replaced by 'God is nice and in Him is no nastiness at all'! This, however, comes a long way short of the Bible view of God's holiness, which we have already considered in the second chapter. God cannot tolerate sin in any form. He cannot possibly co-exist with our sin. So in verse 6 John is underlining the truth that anybody who wants to take an easy-going view of God and a careless attitude towards sin will find that fellowship with God on these terms is impossible. Fellowship with God means sharing God's antagonism to sin.

[1] S. C. Neill, *Christian Holiness* (Lutterworth, 1960), p. 27.

This is why a right attitude towards God lies at the very heart of Christian living and is an essential to spiritual health. It imparts a sense of responsibility to our living.

Secondly, we must beware of underestimating the importance of the principle of sin working within us. In addition to the inadequate views of our sinful nature we considered earlier in this chapter, there are the popular psychological theories which are held in the world. Sin ceases to be sin. Instead of regarding a sinner as a wrongdoer who deserves to be punished, he is regarded as suffering from a disease and deserves our pity. Now, of course, where responsibility begins and ends in some cases can be a great problem. But what we must emphasize here is the need to guard the full biblical doctrine as far as our own lives are concerned. Because, if we are to progress towards the great ideal 'that you may not sin', then it is vital to recognize the solemn facts of our own nature.

Thirdly, we have to avoid the pitfall of saying, 'that we have no sin'. Such a view is serious because, as John points out, it contradicts the very Word of God. There are many ways in which it can be expressed. One is simply through carelessness, just not bothering about the sins that mar and spoil our lives. In many Christians there is a built-in refusal to admit the possibility of being wrong and a desire, if it is possible, to dodge the accusing finger. There are always excuses to shelter behind to remove all sense of guilt. A Christian who would make progress towards the goal before him must pay continual attention to the details of his life, including not only what he does but the words he says, the way he says them and the way he even thinks. He has to be on the look-out for 'the little foxes, that spoil the vineyards' (Song of Solomon 2: 15). He must be willing to face individual and specific sins.

CHAPTER IX

CHRISTIAN GROWTH

I. ITS EMPHASIS IN SCRIPTURE

IF perfection and complete sanctification are not attainable during this life, then we shall not be surprised to discover that one of the features of the Christian life which is very prominent in Scripture is growth. Here is the vital positive truth to put in the place of the error we have sought to expose. It is this feature the apostle Paul so often looks for in the lives of his readers. He urges it, prays for it, and, when there is evidence of it, he thanks God. Here are some examples:

'Rather, speaking the truth in love, we are to grow up in every way into him' (Eph. 4: 15).

'And it is my prayer that your love may abound more and more' (Phil. 1: 9).

'We are bound to give thanks to God always for you, brethren, as is fitting, because your faith is growing abundantly' (2 Thes. 1: 3).

Other New Testament writers express the same desire for their readers. The second Epistle of Peter closes with a call to 'grow in the grace and knowledge of our Lord and Saviour Jesus Christ' (2 Pet. 3: 18). John picks out three particular stages of Christian growth: childhood, young manhood and old age (1 Jn. 2: 12–14), while the writer to the Hebrews says 'Let us . . . go on to maturity' (Heb. 6: 1).

The writers of the New Testament assume that a Christian will make progress in his experience of God and the holiness of his life. There is little to suggest that what is needed is one decisive act of consecration at some time subsequent to one's conversion. This is the mistake that many have made, and it has often led to disillusionment and despair. But as T. C. Hammond has pointed out, 'The whole tenor of Scripture is against the idea that one supreme act of decision secures to us permanently all the blessing of sanctification.'[1] Growth is one of the marks of health in a man's spiritual life, as it is in the physical lives of animals and plants. Indeed lack of growth, or immaturity, is often the cause of defects in some Christians' lives. Inability to use Holy Scripture is one example of this, and the writer to the Hebrews likens the person who lacks progress in this to an unweaned baby (Heb. 5: 11–13). Instability is viewed in the same way, and Paul calls upon us, 'that we may no longer be children, tossed to and fro and carried about with every wind of doctrine, by the cunning of men, by their craftiness in deceitful wiles. Rather, speaking the truth in love, we are to grow up in every way into him who is the head, into Christ' (Eph. 4: 14, 15). The carnal Christians in Corinth are spoken of as 'babes in Christ'; it is spiritual immaturity that lies at the bottom of the divisions for which Paul criticizes them (1 Cor. 3: 1 ff.).

To recognize the importance of growth in the Christian life should lead to one or two practical effects. To the complacent it ought to bring a challenge. If the Christian life is from beginning to end intended to be one of steady growth, those who imagine that they have arrived at some superior state of holiness need to be shaken out of their superiority. This side of heaven there will always be more ground to be possessed, and people who imagine otherwise may be in a rut and have been there for years. On the other hand, for the disheartened, this teaching on growth may come as a great comfort. Those who are deeply conscious of where they fall short, and are discouraged at their apparent lack of spiritual attainment, need to be reminded that in the Christian life everything does not come at once, and that because sanctification is a process, there is the prospect of better things ahead if they will persevere in the proper use of the means of grace.

[1] T. C. Hammond, *The New Creation* (Marshall, Morgan and Scott, 1953), pp. 151 f.

II. THE RESPECTS IN WHICH WE GROW

We must now be more specific and ask the respects in which we grow. First of all, however, there are two ways in which we do not grow. As has been pointed out in chapter VII, there is no growth in our justification before God. Whether a Christian has only just been converted or has believed in Jesus Christ for forty years makes no difference as far as his justification is concerned. This is not a matter of degree. A person is either justified or not justified. He is either an object of God's favour or of His wrath and condemnation. He is like the prisoner in the dock who is either declared 'Guilty' or 'Not Guilty', but never 'Fairly Guilty'. The same can be said of regeneration, the first stage in sanctification. As we saw in chapter VI, a person either possesses spiritual life or he does not, and once a person who has been dead in trespasses and sins has been quickened by the Holy Spirit of God he will never be any more regenerate than he is then. After all, a person of thirty years of age is no more alive than a new-born baby.

On the other hand, the Bible shows that there are certain distinctive aspects of the Christian life in which growth is to be expected. Most of the references to Christian growth have to do with the increase of our faith and love, but there are others, too.

a. Growth in grace (2 Pet. 3 : 18)

A Christian lives in the realm of grace. All he is and hopes for is not according to his own merit or deserving, but is due to the free, unmerited favour of God. So a growing Christian is one who experiences more and more of God's grace and favour.

This is what Peter means when he expresses the wish that grace should 'be multiplied' to his readers (1 Pet. 1 : 2 and 2 Pet. 1 : 2). It is not that he thinks of the grace of God itself as capable of increase, but Peter's prayer is, as Alan Stibbs remarks, 'that his readers may increase in personal experience of the character and benefit of God's dealings with men in Christ and by the Spirit'.[1] This means, of necessity, that a Christian who is growing in his experience of the grace of God will have a correspondingly deepening awareness of the sinfulness of his own nature and his need of God's mercy. Thus the apostle Paul shows his own growth in grace in regarding himself as 'the very least of all the saints' (Eph. 3: 8), and the foremost of sinners (1 Tim. 1: 15). Bishop Ryle observes of the growing Christian: 'The riper he is for glory, the more, like the ripe corn, he hangs down his head. The brighter and clearer is his light, the more he sees of the shortcomings and infirmities of his own heart. When first converted, he would tell you he saw but little of them compared to what he sees now. Would anyone know whether he is growing in grace? Be sure that you look within for increased humility.'[2]

b. Growth in knowledge (2 Pet. 3: 18)

The knowledge to which we refer is, of course, the knowledge of spiritual things and not worldly wisdom. Knowledge of the latter kind merely 'puffs up', as Paul had to remind the Corinthians (1 Cor. 8: 1). Spurgeon once aptly observed: 'Swelling is not growing.' However, there is a knowledge of spiritual things and supremely of God Himself that is an indispensable part of the deepening of our Christian experience. Paul gives as his great aim in life, 'that I may know him' (Phil. 3: 10). Notice that such knowledge is the characteristic mark of the maturity of the apostle John's 'fathers' (1 Jn. 2: 13 f.).

c. Growth in faith

There are many references to this aspect of growth (see, *e.g.*, Lk. 17: 5 f.; 2 Cor. 10: 15; 2 Thes. 1: 3). The strength of our faith has a great deal to do with the extent of our sanctification. Here, incidentally, is a further difference between

[1] A. M. Stibbs, *I Peter* (Tyndale New Testament Commentary, 1959), p. 73.
[2] J. C. Ryle, *Holiness* (James Clarke, 1952), p. 88.

justification and sanctification which we could add to chapter VII. For justification a weak faith is quite sufficient, as John Berridge, an evangelical leader in the eighteenth century, observed in a letter: 'Remember also that salvation does not depend on the *strength* of faith, but the *reality* of it. In the gospels, Jesus often rebukes weak faith, but never rejects it. Weak faith brings but little comfort, yet is as much entitled to salvation as strong.'[1] The man in the Gospels with the demon-possessed boy discovered the truth of this. Basically, he believed in Jesus, but his was a weak faith, and easily hindered by the atmosphere of unbelief in which he lived, and the failure of Christ's disciples. Yet he found when he approached Jesus with the words: 'I believe; help my unbelief', that Jesus granted him his request (Mk. 9: 24). And so it is for justification, for the person whose faith is still at the stage expressed by the hymn, 'I hold Thee with a trembling hand', can be certain that this is enough to bring him peace with God.

But for progress in the Christian life it is a very different story, for then the strength of a person's faith most certainly does matter. We will express this in the precise, theological language of Berkhof: 'While even the weakest faith mediates a perfect justification, the degree of sanctification is commensurate with the strength of the Christian's faith and the persistence with which he apprehends Christ.'[2] There are many examples of such faith in Scripture, such as the long list of Old Testament saints in Hebrews 11. Why was it that these Old Testament men lived such effective lives for God? It was surely because they were men of faith, as we are repeatedly told throughout the chapter. They did not just have the bare minimum of faith whereby they could receive the grace of God, but they were, as we are told in the case of Abraham, 'strong in faith'. How different this is from the theory that justification and sanctification are received by different and separate acts of faith! It is as the faith we already possess

[1] J. C. Ryle, *Five Christian Leaders of the Eighteenth Century* (Banner of Truth, 1960), p. 147.
[2] L. Berkhof, *Systematic Theology* (Banner of Truth, 1959), p. 537.

deepens and grows stronger in response to God's grace that we may progress in the life which God has given us to live.

d. Growth in love

Love is the gift that we are to seek above all others and without it all our Christian activity and good works are useless in God's sight (1 Cor. 13). To be filled with love is the most distinctive mark of Christian maturity (1 Cor. 13: 11), so it is hardly surprising that so many of the references to growth have to do with love (see, e.g., Phil. 1: 9; 1 Thes. 3: 12; 4: 9 f.). Notice, by the way, that this love is not to be an undiscerning charity but should be combined with 'knowledge and all discernment' (Phil. 1: 9).

e. Growth in character and life

Here is the result of all the other aspects of growth, for, as we increase in knowledge, faith and love, so we develop in Christian character and Christlikeness. At the same time, our Christian living and service become increasingly effective and pleasing to God. Paul urges the Thessalonians, 'Finally, brethren, we beseech and exhort you . . . as you learned from us how you ought to live and to please God, just as you are doing, you do so more and more' (1 Thes. 4: 1). We become increasingly like Christ, for we grow 'to the measure of the stature of the fullness of Christ' and 'grow up in every way into him who is the head, into Christ' (Eph. 4: 13, 15). As we daily occupy ourselves with the things of Christ, so we are gradually changed 'into his likeness from one degree of glory to another: for this comes from the Lord who is the Spirit' (2 Cor. 3: 18).

III. THE NATURE OF GROWTH

There are two things to be said about the nature of growth.

a. A Christian grows in response to God's grace

Why is the Christian life one of progress? Is it because God's blessing is held back and only given to us in degrees? We have the answer to this in Ephesians 1, where we read that God has 'blessed us in Christ with every spiritual blessing in the heavenly places' (Eph. 1: 3). This is an accomplished fact. If we have Christ then we have everything God has for us and He has held nothing back. To keep to Ephesians for the moment, what we need is not for God to give us anything that He has held back, but rather to be made aware of all that is ours in Christ and then fully to appropriate it. It is for this that Paul prays in this Epistle. In the first prayer in chapter 1 he seeks a greater awareness of all that God has done, together with the enlightenment which this demands (Eph. 1: 15–23). Then in the second prayer (Eph. 3: 16–21), he goes on to pray for a full experience of all this through the indwelling of Jesus Christ by His Spirit. It is on this basis that the Christian life is to be lived. So, having shown in the first three chapters the greatness of our calling in Christ and the wonder of it all, he introduces the practical section at the beginning of chapter 4 with the words: 'I . . . beg you to lead a life worthy of the calling to which you have been called.' One can readily detect echoes of the Ephesian Epistle in the words of H. W. Cragg: 'Our contention then is well-founded when we stress the importance of a comprehensive view of our salvation. There can be no subdividing of Christ, and whatever sub-divisions are needed in our consideration of Him must be due to the slowness of our hearts to grasp, or our minds to comprehend, all the fullness that we have in Him.'[1] We have found here an answer to our question. The Christian needs to grow because of the imperfect way in which he has understood and responded to the gospel and all its implications. This is clear in the various aspects of a Christian's growth we have already discovered from Scripture. Most of them are in some way a growth in response to God and His truth. For example, we grow in knowledge as we devote ourselves to the truth which God has revealed. Faith is our response to God's grace, while our love is our response to His love, for 'We love, because he first loved us' (1 Jn. 4: 19).

[1] H. W. Cragg, *The Conqueror's Way* (IVF, 1949), p. 23.

It is his deficient response to Jesus Christ that Paul writes about in Philippians 3: 12, 'Not that I have already obtained this or am already perfect; but I press on to make it my own, because Christ Jesus has made me his own.' Notice that Paul here confesses that despite all that God has thus far done in his life, and even though Christ has taken the initiative and fully laid hold of him (*i.e.*, 'Christ Jesus has made me his own'), he himself has not fully 'obtained', or laid hold of everything that Christ has for him. J. B. Phillips makes Paul's meaning especially clear. He translates it as, 'Yet, my brothers, I do not consider myself to have "arrived", spiritually, nor do I consider myself already perfect. But I keep going on, grasping even more firmly that purpose for which Christ Jesus grasped me. My brothers, I do not consider myself to have fully grasped it even now. But I do concentrate on this: I leave the past behind and with hands outstretched to whatever lies ahead I go straight for the goal—my reward the honour of my high calling by God in Christ Jesus' (Phil. 3: 12-14).

Mercifully, by God's grace, as we have seen above, we can be justified through an imperfect faith (and who of us would dare to claim that our faith is perfect?), but we must never rest content with this. We should be like Paul who said: 'I press on to make it my own, because Christ Jesus has made me his own.' Early in the chapter he has gloried in his spiritual *position*. 'But when he comes to speak of his spiritual *condition* the possessing thought is that all is imperfect and progressive. He has a perfect blessing; but he is an imperfect recipient of it; he has "not attained".'[1]

Now all this has a most important bearing on the kind of claims Christians are entitled to make concerning their spiritual attainments. In view of the considerations above it is surely inappropriate for any Christian to suggest that he has made a *perfect* or *complete* response to the grace of God. Claims to have *fully* surrendered or yielded one's life to God have no counterparts in the pages of Holy Scripture; in view of what

[1] H. C. G. Moule, *Philippian Studies* (Pickering and Inglis, 1956), p. 189.

Paul says in the passage we have just studied, it is hard to imagine that he would have ever made them. It is because of his awareness of his deficiencies that Paul has no satisfaction in the stage of progress he has reached. Instead, like an athlete intent on reaching the winning tape, he strains every nerve and sinew, 'straining forward to what lies ahead, I press on towards the goal for the prize of the upward call of God in Christ Jesus' (Phil. 3: 13, 14).

b. A Christian grows from within

The word mostly used for the growth of a Christian in the New Testament is *auxano*, which is the word normally used of organic growth. In other words, a Christian grows from within as a living organism. John Owen observes the way in which Scripture so frequently likens the Christian's growth in grace and holiness to the growth of trees and plants. Here is one of the comparisons he makes: 'These trees and plants have the principle of their growth in themselves. They do not grow immediately from external adventitious aid, but from their own seminal virtue and radical moisture. It is no otherwise in the progress of holiness; it has a root, a seed, a principle of growth in the soul. All grace is immortal seed, and contains in it a living growing principle, John 4: 14. That which has not in itself a life and power of growth, is not grace. And therefore whatever duties men perform, as directed by natural light, or urged by convictions from the word, if they proceed not from a principle of spiritual life in the heart, they are not fruits of holiness.'[1] It is important to notice the depth at which a Christian grows. It is not just a matter of forming fresh habits in life, although this may well have to take place. Rather, Christian growth is internal and springs from the innermost being of the Christian where the Holy Spirit of God is at work. Growth which is nothing more than the forming of fresh habits could be like tying fruit to the branches of a tree—utterly superficial.

This leads on naturally to another comparison which John

[1] J. Owen, *On the Holy Spirit* (1674), p. 237.

Owen makes: 'The growth of trees and plants is secret and imperceptible, and discerned only in the effects and consequences of it; the most watchful eye can discern little of its motion; and so it is in the progress of holiness. It is not immediately discernible either by those in whom it is, or by others who observe it, except by its fruits and effects.'[1]

Now let us apply all this to the way in which a Christian's faith grows. It is shown very strikingly in Luke 17: 5, 6. The apostles, having recognized the importance of their faith, ask the Lord, 'Increase our faith!' The Greek word for 'increase' is significant. It is not *auxano* but *prostithemi*. This may imply that they were asking our Lord to add to their faith in the way bricks are added to a building by someone, externally. It may just mean 'Grant us faith'. Whichever is the case, there is no uncertainty about Jesus' reply. He spoke of faith in organic terms, likening true faith to a grain of mustard seed: 'If you had faith as a grain of mustard seed, you could say to this sycamine tree, "Be rooted up, and be planted in the sea," and it would obey you.' True faith may be very small like a grain of mustard seed, but it possesses life with all its possibilities. Dr. Campbell Morgan illustrates this by the story of a remarkable tomb he saw somewhere in Italy. Its occupant had left instructions in his will that a large mass of granite should be laid over it, so that if there was ever a resurrection, it would not affect him! As it happened, an acorn was dropped by a bird just before the block was lowered. Eventually the acorn germinated and grew. Such was the power of the life within it, that the stone was split in two and an oak tree grew up through the crack and gradually separated the two halves of granite. If our faith is like that, if it is more than a dead orthodoxy, if it is living, then it possesses enormous potentialities, and can move mountains, however small it may appear to be.

IV. MEANS OF GRACE

If Christian growth is organic, then it needs the right food and

[1] J. Owen, *On the Holy Spirit* (1674), p. 237.

the right conditions. This was why Dr. Campbell Morgan's acorn germinated, for it had underneath the slab of granite just the warmth and moisture it needed. What does Christian growth require? Surely, the supreme need is for the food of God's Word. 'Long for the pure spiritual milk,' writes Peter, 'that by it you may grow' (1 Pet. 2: 2). Lack of knowledge of God's truth is one of the most common causes of immaturity and instability. Notice how these two conditions are brought together when Peter speaks of those who are 'ignorant and unstable' (2 Pet. 3: 16). Here is what Thomas Watson (he was the seventeenth-century minister of St. Stephen's, Walbrook, until he was ejected under the Act of Uniformity) has to say about this: 'Such as are unlearned in the main points of divinity are unstable. As the body cannot be strong that has the sinews shrunk; so neither can that Christian be strong in religion who wants the grounds of knowledge, which are the sinews to strengthen and stablish him.'[1] The immature and unstable Christian does not necessarily need to make some specific act of consecration (although some may do so, as we shall see in our next chapter), but may well be simply in need of teaching. It means, too, that when a Christian reads his Bible, he ought to take a long-term view. He is not merely looking for a thought to help him through the next twenty-four hours (although if it so happens that what he reads has particular application to his circumstances at the time, this is all to the good), but primarily he is deepening his understanding of God and His ways with men as revealed in the Bible, and in consequence seeing to it that his whole life and outlook are moulded by this. At the same time, of course, he must see to it that he makes immediate response to everything he learns from the Bible. As James shows, this is the way of not being a forgetful hearer if we are 'doers of the word, and not hearers only' (Jas. 1: 22 ff.).

A great deal depends also on the attitude of mind with which we go through life. In the passage in Philippians 3, to which we have already referred, Paul reveals something of the

[1] T. Watson, *A Body of Divinity* (Banner of Truth, 1958), p. 4.

way in which he sets about taking a firmer hold of all that Christ has for him. To begin with, he describes his quest as '*one* thing I do', the very opposite of the diffusion against which the apostle James warns us: 'a double-minded man (is) unstable in all his ways' (Jas. 1: 8). Paul is not going to fall into that trap and so his whole life is unified around the one purpose of pressing 'toward the goal' at which he is aiming.

Paul also reveals that he is forward-looking. 'Forgetting what lies behind and straining forward to what lies ahead' (Phil. 3: 13). There are some great blessings in the former part of his life to which he has already referred in the chapter, but he does not allow these to make him complacent and to rest content with what he already has. He is like the athlete whose eye is fixed on the winning tape. He also says, 'I press on toward the goal', and the verb here is one used in hunting and is also used of the athlete who strains every nerve to achieve his object. This is the attitude by which the growing Christian will feed himself on the Word of God. He will do so with determination and will refuse to give up at any difficulties he encounters, whether in himself or in the Bible he is studying. He will recognize, as Paul described to the converts of his first missionary journey, that he often 'through many tribulations . . . must enter the kingdom of God' (Acts 14: 22).

Indeed trials and difficulties are regarded as means of grace. It is always assumed in Scripture that the Christian life is lived in a world which is not conducive to spiritual life. A Christian is to expect persecution and tribulation and in this he is simply following in the steps of his Master. God uses these experiences to develop Christian character. Indeed, without them a Christian may be like a greenhouse plant that has never been hardened. Look, for example, at Romans 5: 3–5, where, because of the way the trials of life can be to a Christian's profit, Paul is able to claim, 'we rejoice in our sufferings'. We see the same kind of effect in James 1: 2–4.

One way in which we can benefit from our trials is in the matter of our faith, as this example from James shows. 'The testing of your faith' means that our faith is like a precious metal which needs to be refined and purified from dross. Sometimes our faith is marred by biases and prejudices. Often it is vague, or softened by shallow sentimentality. Yet, as we have seen in this chapter, it is vital to our sanctification. How, then, is it to be refined? Often it is by the refining fires of persecution or other forms of tribulation. And faith, if it is real, like a metal will come to no harm. Only the dross will be burned away 'that the genuineness of your faith, more precious than gold which though perishable is tested by fire, may redound to praise and glory and honour at the revelation of Jesus Christ' (1 Pet. 1: 7).

CHAPTER X

CRISES ON THE WAY

THE Christian life, then, normally makes progress by steady growth, and this is what Scripture encourages us to expect, as we saw in the last chapter. What then do we make of the Christian who claims to have experienced a sudden and decisive change subsequent to his conversion, perhaps at a convention or because of some crisis in his circumstances, which has resulted in his Christian life being victorious to a far greater degree than before?

Now an experience of this kind is not necessarily incompatible with the steady growth which, as we saw in the last chapter, is a prominent feature of the Christian life. It is feasible that there will be times in a Christian's life when he will make more progress than at other times as the result perhaps of a meeting or service he has attended or a particularly helpful book he has read. These are like the 'sudden gusts and motions' and the 'intense vigorous actings of grace on great occasions', for which John Owen allows;[1] they are like the opening of buds and flowers. What can be misleading, however, is the habit of some in referring to such experiences as '*The* Second Blessing'. They assume such an experience to be a normal part of every Christian's life, and think that any Christian who has not had it ought to seek it because it is essential to living the Christian life as God intended it to be lived. As a result, some Christians have often been put through unnecessary anxiety in trying to get an experience they were probably never intended to have.

Now it is usually a good thing to remember that Christian experience is not necessarily the same thing as the experience of some Christians! By this we do not mean that any sudden turning-point in a Christian's life is to be regarded as spurious.

[1] J. Owen, *On the Holy Spirit* (1674), p. 238.

Trying to explain away parts of other Christians' testimonies is rarely a profitable pursuit, and unbelievers are often masters of it. What we are saying, however, is that whereas such experiences may be perfectly valid for the person who has them, they are never meant to be regarded as the norm for all Christians. Still less are other Christians to be urged to seek such crises for themselves. Some booklets and tracts have fallen into this error. In them the author fills most of the space writing about himself and his experience. He tells us how his life had been defeated and lacking in blessing, and how he went through some experience which affected a change in his life and led him to greater victory. He then interprets Scripture in the light of his experience and seeks to press it on all Christians. Surely the ground for what we believe about the Christian life is the Bible and not another man's experience, and the only kind of experience we have any right to press on others is what is clearly shown in Scripture.

For one thing, there are many who fail to understand their own experience. They speak of being 'blessed', but are not always able to be more specific than this. Sometimes any upsurge of emotion in a meeting is regarded as evidence of 'blessing'. It is quite possible to experience considerable relief on conquering one's embarrassment at staying to an after-meeting and to feel, in consequence, that one has been 'blessed'. The only safe thing to do is to interpret all these experiences in the light of Scripture and not vice versa. Judged by this standard some examples of 'Second Blessing' would more accurately be described as conversion. This is especially likely, for example, in those who have made professions of conversion under a shallow evangelistic ministry in which there is little more than an appeal to 'come to Jesus' with no mention of repentance. It is interesting to notice that Bishop Ryle made this same observation in the Introduction to his book on holiness: 'Are they not, when they urge on believers the "higher life" as a second conversion, underrating the length, and breadth, and depth, and height, of that great first change which Scripture calls the new birth, the new creation, the spiritual resurrection? I may be mistaken. But I have sometimes thought, while reading the strong language used by many about "consecration", in the last few years, that those who use it must have had previously a singularly low and inadequate view of "conversion", if indeed they knew anything about conversion at all. In short, I have almost suspected that when they were *consecrated*, they were in reality *converted* for the first time!'[1]

One of the ways in which conversion has been belittled by some Christians has been the attempt to separate 'accepting Jesus as Saviour' and 'accepting Jesus as Lord'. It has often been suggested that the latter is a second experience subsequent to conversion. Yet is this really scriptural? Do we ever find New Testament writers urging on their readers the need to accept Christ as Lord? The assumption is that this has already taken place at conversion. This, for example, is how Paul spoke of the Christian life, 'As therefore you received Christ Jesus the Lord, so live in him, rooted and built up in him and established in the faith, just as you were taught, abounding in thanksgiving' (Col. 2 : 6, 7). The early Christians would have been quite surprised to hear 'Jesus is Lord' as a second experience. For them it was a baptismal confession! So Paul's appeal to the Colossians is not 'As therefore you have had a second experience, so live in accordance with that', but he looks back to their conversion as setting the tone for their Christian living.

Most Christians, of course, who can look back on many years of Christian discipleship can detect a number of points at which God seemed to speak to them in some special way and, as a result, were able to make a big step forward in their Christian progress. It may be that when these stages of Christian growth are compared, one stands out above the others, both in its depth and the effect it has had on the person's life. Yet this does not mean that we have here a second experience which is the norm for every Christian.

Whenever we see challenges in God's Word, our response

should be immediate and decisive. This seems to be the reason why the aorist imperative is so often used in the New Testament. Is there a sin to forsake? Then this calls for a definite act of repentance. So the Laodicean church were called to repent with an aorist imperative, although they were commanded to 'be zealous' in the present imperative, which implies a continuing attitude (Rev. 3: 19). A decisive response is called for in the words of Jesus: 'If your right hand causes you to sin, cut it off and throw it away' (Mt. 5: 30). As James Philip realizes, 'That is crisis enough in the believer's experience, in that it demands drastic action to put matters right, just as, in the sphere of medicine, appendicitis is a "crisis" requiring immediate surgical intervention to safeguard life and health. But this drastic "crisis-action" in the spiritual realm is therapeutic, and in one very important sense only preparatory to the real business of Christian growth. It removes the hindrance to growth, and makes it possible, but it is not the growth itself, just as surgery removes the cause of illness, and makes possible better health in the future.'[1] The same could be said of other types of response for which God's Word often calls.

However, a word of caution is called for here. Whereas the use of the aorist does imply a decisive step of obedience to God's Word, we are not entitled to build on this a doctrine of a once-for-all crisis of surrender subsequent to conversion. An example often quoted in this connection is the use of the aorist tense for 'yield yourselves' in Romans 6: 13. It is often claimed that this must refer to a single crisis in the Christian life through which every Christian must at some time pass if he is to live a victorious Christian life. If this system of interpretation is followed throughout the New Testament whenever an aorist imperative is encountered, some very curious theories could be produced! What, for example, are we to do with the succession of aorists in 2 Timothy 4: 2, 'Preach the word, be urgent in season and out of season, convince, rebuke and exhort'? 'Repent' is usually in the aorist tense in the New Testament, including Revelation 3: 19, where it is addressed

[1] J. Philip, *Christian Maturity* (IVF, 1964), p. 58.

to church members. This, however, does not entitle us to teach a once-for-all crisis of repentance subsequent to conversion any more than 'everyone must have his appendix removed before true health is possible'.[1] We have, of course, to decide from the context whether a once-for-all act is implied, and there is nothing to suggest in Romans 6 that this is what Paul had in mind here. Perhaps an illustration will help at this point. I may say to my little boy, 'Eat up your dinner', and if I were speaking in the Greek of the New Testament, I might well use an aorist imperative because I want him to make a definite act of obedience. I could not, however, mean that this one act of obedience will be enough to last him the rest of his life! It is quite likely that whenever he is confronted with something to eat I will say the same thing in the same way. So it is with the command to yield in Romans 6. It does not say, 'Yield yourselves to God and you will then live a life of constant victory', although there are other verses in the New Testament where the aorist imperative is used in this way. Look, for example, at Acts 16: 31, where there is a definite consequence following from a decisive act of faith. Rather the meaning in Romans 6 is that whenever one is faced with a choice between yielding our members 'instruments of wickedness' or 'instruments of righteousness', we are to do the latter and to do it decisively.[2]

SOME EXAMPLES OF 'SECOND BLESSING'

What then are some of those experiences subsequent to conversion which seem to stand out above others? We do not claim that the following list is exhaustive, but we refer to some which are frequently encountered.

[1] J. Philip, *Christian Maturity* (IVF, 1964), p. 59.
[2] It is worth mentioning that G. C. Neal in an article, 'In the Original Greek', published in the *Tyndale House Bulletin*, April 1963, has strongly questioned the whole idea of what he calls 'the supposed distinction between the present and aorist tenses of the Greek verb in the infinitive, imperative, and subjunctive'.

a. Recovery from backsliding

In view of what we have said about the full implication of conversion in the Bible, it is not surprising that some outstanding experiences in the Christian life are, in effect, a recovery from backsliding from all that a believer possessed in Christ at his conversion. It is interesting to notice that the writers of two recent booklets come to the same conclusion, although by somewhat different routes.

James Philip asserts: 'According to the Scriptures, conversion and consecration are simultaneous, in the sense that no conversion ever really takes place that does not mean, imply and involve, a true consecration to Christ. One does not give part of one's allegiance to Christ at conversion, then at a later stage make a complete surrender to Him, called consecration. One does not enter into the kingdom at all except on terms of unconditional surrender.'[1] However, Christians can and often do fall away from these terms on which they started the Christian life, so James Philip continues: 'A believer may lose the keen edge of his consecration and fall away from that attitude of total commitment which marked his entrance into the kingdom of God. If he does so, then a new consecration is necessary, and sometimes this is quite as clear-cut and decisive —and sudden—as a conversion experience, a crisis indeed, if this is the word to be used to describe it. But it is necessary to be clear about what has happened. It is not an advance to another stage of experience so much as a return to a previous one. A great deal depends on a true realization of this. For obviously, if a believer does not fall away from his first consecration, but follows on to know the Lord ever more deeply, he does not require to renew it again (except in so far as our consecration is renewed day by day, and hour by hour, which is not the point at issue here).'

The other booklet to which we refer is devoted to the work of the Holy Spirit. In this, J. R. W. Stott shows that since Pentecost the full blessings of the Holy Spirit are given at conversion, for the Holy Spirit is the distinctive blessing of the

[1] J. Philip, *Christian Maturity* (IVF, 1964), p. 56 f.

new age, and it is universal and continuous. A person receives
the Holy Spirit in His abundance by coming to Jesus, that is,
by believing in Him (Jn. 7: 37 ff.).[1] What, then, do we make
of Christians who by the poverty of their lives show so little
evidence of the work of the Holy Spirit? Here is how J. R. W.
Stott accounts for this: 'But the backslidings of Christians are
evidence of their need, not to be baptized with the Spirit (even
the proud, loveless, quarrelsome and sin-tolerant Corinthian
Christians had been baptized with the Spirit; see 1 Cor. 12:
13), but to recover the fullness of the Spirit, which they have
lost through sin, thus becoming what the Corinthian Christians were, namely "unspiritual" or "carnal" (1 Cor. 3: 1 ff.).
It is in this sense that many Christians do have an experience
in two stages or more. It is not the general will and purpose of
God (which is a continuous and increasing appropriation); it
is due rather to their sinful backsliding.'[2] The writer shows
that the initial, unrepeatable reception of the Holy Spirit is
sometimes denoted by the term 'baptized with the Spirit',
whereas the fullness of the Holy Spirit relates to the continuing
experience: 'The baptism was a unique initiatory experience;
the fullness was intended to be the continuing, the permanent
result, the norm. (See Acts 6: 3; 7: 55; 11: 24; 13: 52 and Lk.
1: 15, 41, 67). As an initiatory event the baptism is not repeat-
able and cannot be lost, but the filling can be repeated and in
any case needs to be maintained. If it is not maintained, it is
lost. If it is lost, it can be recovered. The Holy Spirit is
"grieved" by sin (Eph. 4: 30) and ceases to fill the sinner.
Repentance is then the only road to recovery.' We feel justified in assuming, then, that if the members of the church at
Ephesus heeded the charge, 'you have abandoned the love you
had at first' (Rev. 2: 4), this would have involved them in a
decisive turning-point in their Christian lives.

Again, however, we must emphasize that this experience

---

[1] For a helpful explanation of these verses see J. R. W. Stott, *The
Baptism and Fullness of the Holy Spirit* (IVF, 1964), p. 21 ff.
[2] J. R. W. Stott, *The Baptism and Fullness of the Holy Spirit* (IVF,
1964), p. 25.

should not be imposed indiscriminately on every Christian. The fullness of the Spirit is represented in Scripture as an abiding experience. It is indeed noteworthy that the only place in Scripture where Christians are commanded, 'Be filled with the Spirit'[1] (Eph. 5: 18), this is expressed with a present imperative, which implies that here is a state of affairs which has to be maintained from day to day.

b. A crisis of discovery

Sometimes great blessings attend the re-discovery of a neglected truth. Was not this the experience of Paul when God said to him, 'My grace is sufficient for you' (2 Cor. 12: 9)? Many other Christians, too, have lived for years without a full realization of all that these words imply of the sufficiency of Christ to meet every need.[2] Others have had what might be described as a 'Calvinistic second blessing'! For many Christians look back warmly on their discovery of the sovereignty of God and other truths connected with it. Verses like 'You did not choose me, but I chose you' (Jn. 15: 16) have filled them with a sense of wonder at the grace of God, that He should take the initiative in bringing them to a knowledge of salvation in Jesus Christ. They have come to realize that by nature they were dead in sin and utterly blind to the things of God, and that they would still be in that condition if God had not commanded the light of the gospel to shine into their darkened hearts (see 2 Cor. 4: 6). They can now sing Charles Wesley's words with fresh understanding:

'Long my imprisoned spirit lay
    Fast bound in sin and nature's night;
Thine eye diffused a quickening ray,—
    I woke, the dungeon flamed with light;
My chains fell off, my heart was free,
I rose, went forth, and followed Thee.'

[1] For a treatment of this topic, see Leon Morris, *Spirit of the Living God* (IVF, 1960), pp. 89 ff.

[2] This truth seems to have made a big impact on some of the early leaders of the 'Keswick' movement.

c. An awareness of the cost of discipleship

To live the Christian life is a costly matter. Yet this is not always faced at first. Many who have had the privilege of a Christian home have found it easy to make a Christian profession, perhaps less costly than resisting the gospel! Others may have entered the kingdom of God in a camp or house-party for young people where everyone was professing conversion. It was, of course, in circumstances like these that Jesus made a special point of emphasizing the cost of discipleship. We read: 'And there went great multitudes with him; and he turned, and said unto them . . .', then follows the statement on the cost of Christian discipleship. Apparently, Jesus saw the danger inherent in circumstances in which it had almost become the fashion to follow after Him. However, in these days, this important piece of teaching is not always emphasized as it should be, and when it is stressed it may not have quite the impact that is needed. So for a time the young Christian is oblivious to some of the real issues. Then he goes out into the world and there is a painful awakening in store. To live the Christian life is no longer the easy thing it was in the shelter of a Christian home, or perhaps in a school where reasonable standards of decency were observed. To be a Christian now involves going against the stream, being thought odd, and often ridiculed for one's faith and the standard one seeks to maintain. This may have a chilling effect on the zeal of a Christian, and the issues of discipleship have to be faced again, this time with the cost in view. Such an experience can involve a real crisis and perhaps the spiritual prospects of the person are, from the point of view of human observation, in the balance for a period.

d. 'Full assurance'

There is a difference between a faith which is enough for salvation, and that which is sufficient for full assurance, and not every Christian has the latter. It is for this that we are to seek diligently (Heb. 6: 11), and is the manner in which it is desirable to approach God in prayer (Heb. 10: 22). We are to use our Bibles to this end, for many are the assurances of God's Word, and one writer distinctly says: 'I write this to you . . . that you may know' (1 Jn. 5: 13). The same Epistle from which we have just quoted gives many assuring evidences that are to be looked for in the life of the Christian believer. Above all, it is the Holy Spirit Himself who imparts the inward certainty to the heart of the believer. We will quote one of the key passages to this topic in full:

'For you did not receive the spirit of slavery to fall back into fear, but you have received the spirit of sonship. When we cry, "Abba! Father!" it is the Spirit himself bearing witness with our spirit that we are children of God, and if children, then heirs, heirs of God and fellow heirs with Christ, provided we suffer with him in order that we may also be glorified with him' (Rom. 8: 15–17).

Now this can often come as an experience subsequent to conversion. It is not necessarily sudden in its effect, but is nonetheless a clearly discernible step in the progress of a Christian. 'Such a fact is constantly asserted by the saints throughout the centuries. They declare that the Holy Spirit made them so certain of the reality and presence of the Lord Jesus Christ and His love for them, that they were more certain of that than of any other fact whatsoever.'[1]

e. Crises of guidance

Although not coming strictly under the heading of sanctification, a young person's discovery of God's will for his life and his appropriate action can indeed be a decisive step, with far-reaching effects in the quality of his life. Sometimes such a decision can follow a long period of conflict and struggle until there is a willingness to do God's will. Perhaps the experience of Jonah could be cited as an example of this.

f. Special gifts of the Holy Spirit

Christians sometimes make claims of having had an experience of the Holy Spirit which has led to their exercising special

[1] D. M. Lloyd-Jones, *Authority* (IVF, 1958), p. 78.

gifts, such as tongues. It is not within the scope of this book to assess these claims.[1] However, there is one relevant point to make here, and it is that such experiences do not have any *necessary direct* connection with sanctification. Notice that we choose our words carefully here, because the experiences we are now considering may have an important *indirect* effect on a person's holiness. For example, they may help in the matter of assurance, which has a real bearing on the way a Christian lives. However, what we are stressing is that there is no necessary connection between the two. We have a clear example of this in the Corinthian church. They were particularly well endowed with gifts of the Holy Spirit, as Paul points out; 'so that you are not lacking in any spiritual gift' (*charisma*) (1 Cor. 1: 7). Yet, for all that, they had not for the most part progressed to any high degree of sanctification, and Paul in the third chapter describes them as 'carnal' and not 'spiritual'. Paul 'makes it clear that the evidence of the Spirit's fullness is not the exercise of His gifts (of which they had plenty), but the ripening of His fruit (of which they had little).'[2] So a Christian may even possess a gift as high on the list in 1 Corinthians 12 as that of teaching, and in consequence be in great demand for addressing meetings, and yet, at the same time, may have advanced little in holiness of life and in the fullness of the Spirit.

How then shall we summarize this chapter? That Christians do have crises no-one can deny. And there is no question that they can often be beneficial. What we have tried to do is to interpret them in the light of Scripture instead of vice versa, as so many do. As a result, we shall not fall into the error of insisting that every Christian needs a crisis experience subsequent to conversion. Then, too, we must observe the way these crises vary. We have mentioned only a few and no doubt readers can add to the list. It brings home to us that every

[1] For a treatment of this, see J. R. W. Stott, *The Baptism and Fullness of the Holy Spirit* (IVF, 1964).

[2] J. R W. Stott, *The Baptism and Fullness of the Holy Spirit* (IVF, 1964), p. 26.

Christian is an individual who has been shaped by his particular, spiritual environment. The teaching he has received is likely to include deficiencies. Some have not been warned of the cost of being a Christian. Others have never realized that faith in Christ involves complete consecration to Him, while there are others who have never appreciated the sufficiency which is theirs in Christ. Or perhaps the true nature of sin and its seriousness have not been properly faced. As a man progresses in the Christian life and these deficiencies are made up, the discovery may well be sudden and with dramatic results, so although the Christian life is normally presented in the New Testament as a steady growth and progress there may well be 'crises on the way'.

CHAPTER XI

FAITH AND EFFORT

WE must now turn to a consideration of man's part in the sanctifying process. This immediately brings before us two possibilities: faith and effort; or, to use two other words often employed, surrender and striving. Here, of course, we have two very different emphases, often denoted by the terms 'quietism' and 'pietism'.

QUIETISM

Quietism is a somewhat mystical view, originally popular among the Quakers, and has been taken over by some of the forms of perfectionism we were dealing with in chapter VIII. The work of sanctification, we are told, does not involve any effort on our part. Indeed, our striving and effort can even be a hindrance to our sanctification. Our part is simply to surrender ourselves to God and to leave Him to give us a life of victory over sin. This is usually regarded as a crisis experience subsequent to conversion, although it must be maintained as a daily attitude on the part of the Christian believer. While we are in this attitude of surrender, we live victoriously. We fall into sin only when we cease to trust completely. Various words such as 'yield', 'surrender' and 'abandonment' are employed, while a catchy phrase which has often been used is 'Let go, let God'.[1] Two lines of a hymn express the idea clearly:

[1] This expression seems to have been first used by C. H. A. Trumbull in a tract entitled *What is your kind of Christianity?* He used it to distinguish between surrender and faith and maintained that we may 'let go' and yet not 'let God'. So the surrendered life is not necessarily a victorious life. These two categories seem to come from Trumbull's imagination rather than from Scripture.

'Holiness by faith in Jesus,
Not by effort of my own.'

The clear implication in these lines is that the Christian has to choose between faith and effort, and the way of holiness is to choose faith.

Sometimes this teaching can be expressed in the most extreme language. Verses like Galatians 2: 20, and especially the phrase 'Not I, but Christ', are taken right out of their context to suggest that a Christian's personality is to be virtually obliterated and replaced by that of Christ. C. H. A. Trumbull often wrote, in books and tracts, in language of this kind. 'The simple fact is', we are told, 'that whenever a life that trusts Christ as Saviour is completely surrendered to Christ as Master, Christ is ready then to take complete control of that life, and at once to fill it with Himself. . . . When we surrender and trust completely we die to self and Christ can and does literally replace our self with Himself. Thus it is no longer we that live but Christ liveth in us in His Person, literally fills our whole being with Himself in actual, personal presence; and He does this not as a figure of speech, but just as literally as that we fill our clothes with ourselves.'[1] In this condition a Christian does not even experience temptation, for it is, as Trumbull puts it, 'defeated by Christ before it has time to draw us into a fight'—if, as B. B. Warfield adds, 'there is any "us" left to be drawn'! This language is strongly reminiscent of that employed by Madame Guyon, the best known of the quietists of the early eighteenth century. Needless to say, all these ideas go far beyond Scripture, and in any case it is very hard to know what precisely they mean in practice. It is quite remarkable to notice the space devoted by some writers to explain what they mean by 'surrender' and other words in their terminology. If these words represent biblical concepts one would expect a little more attention given to them in the Bible itself!

---

[1] I am indebted to B. B. Warfield, *Perfectionism* (PRPC, 1958), p. 381, for this quotation.

A MAJOR OBJECTION

Quite apart from the extremes that we have just referred to, there is a major difficulty to the whole theory which has never really been answered. It is the problem of whose fault it is when a Christian sins—the supporters of this view usually admit that there is such a possibility. Whose fault is it, then? It is hardly the Christian's fault, because when he surrenders himself to God, He then assumes responsibility. At the same time, we rightly shrink from any suggestion that the fault lies with God Himself. One way of answering the problem is to say that a Christian sins only because he has ceased to trust or has left the position of self-surrender, by which he placed himself completely in the hands of God. But this does not answer the difficulty at all, for this ceasing to trust in God is in itself a sin and we are still left with the question, Whose fault, then, is it that the Christian has ceased to trust? How can a Christian, who has handed his life over to God, ever sin again?

Very often when exponents of these theories encounter objections they try to think up some ingenious analogy. Mrs. Pearsall Smith chooses that of the potter and the clay. Now, admittedly, this analogy is used in the pages of Scripture itself, but her use of it goes far beyond what we find in Jeremiah. Here is how she puts it: 'What can be said about man's part in this great work, but that he must continually surrender himself and continually trust? But when we come to God's side of the question, what is there that may not be said as to the manifold and wonderful ways in which He accomplishes the work entrusted to Him? It is here that the growing comes in. The lump of clay could never grow into a beautiful vessel if it stayed in the clay-pit for thousands of years; but when it is put into the hands of a skilful potter it grows rapidly, under his fashioning, into the vessel he intends it to be. And in the same way the soul, abandoned to the working of the Heavenly Potter, is made into a vessel unto honour, sanctified, and meet for the Master's use.'[1]

[1] Mrs. Hannah Pearsall Smith, *The Christian's Secret of a Happy Life* (Nisbet, 1888), p. 34.

Why, then, do things go wrong? Here is how Mrs. Pearsall Smith accounts for this in a lady who had 'lost all her blessing': 'She had understood her part of trusting to begin with, but, not understanding the Divine process of accomplishing that for which she had trusted, she took herself out of the hands of the Heavenly Potter, and the vessel was marred on the wheel.'[1] So one moment a Christian is like a piece of malleable clay, completely soft and without any will of its own, and the next moment like a piece of clay that decides to jump out of the potter's hand. Some clay!

Much as we realize the inadequacies of the quietist point of view, we must have some sympathy with one of its main motives, which is a genuine attempt to stress that 'Salvation is of the Lord'. It has sought to show that man is just as incapable of bringing about his sanctification as his justification. At the same time, it has recognized the complete sufficiency of what God has done for us in Christ for our sanctification as much as for any other aspect of salvation. 'I can't, Christ can' is the way in which it has sometimes been expressed. So all that a Christian can do is passively to let God do everything. While this state of affairs continues, the work of sanctification will proceed and the Christian will live a victorious life. Everything depends on a Christian maintaining his surrender to Christ and abiding in Him. Here is the very point at which the whole theory fails in what it sets out to do; sanctification depends not on God at all but on man and the maintenance of his surrender; not on the potter but on the clay.

Another drawback to this kind of teaching is the uniform type of personality it tends to produce. This, of course, need not surprise us, as Dr. Lloyd-Jones has pointed out: 'If we are to do nothing but just give in and not exert ourselves and our powers, obviously we shall all conform to a certain type and to a certain pattern—the difference between Peter and Paul and John and James will vanish, and Calvin and Luther and Bunyan, and Jonathan Edwards and George Whitefield will

[1] Mrs. Hannah Pearsall Smith, *The Christian's Secret of a Happy Life* (Nisbet, 1888), p. 35.

become identical in the common absence of certain things
from their lives.'[1]

THE PLACE OF EFFORT

To set faith against effort is a false antithesis which is never
made in Scripture. Certainly faith is necessary in sanctification.
We have already stressed the importance of this, and shown
that the degree and depth of our faith bear direct relationship
to the extent of our growth in sanctification (see chapter IX),
but this does not preclude effort. A person who is being renewed by the Holy Spirit is not in a state of passive surrender,
but is actively engaged in mortifying the flesh and putting on
the new man (see chapter XIII). The Christian life is described
as a race (Heb. 12: 1), and as a fight (Eph. 6: 10–18; 1 Tim.
6: 12) and both of these analogies surely imply effort on the
part of the Christian. We have to 'be careful to apply (ourselves) to good deeds' (Tit. 3: 8). The devil is an enemy to be
resisted (Jas. 4: 7). Paul finds it necessary to 'pommel my body
and subdue it, lest after preaching to others I myself should be
disqualified' (1 Cor. 9: 27).[2] Much is often made of the 'rest of
faith' of Hebrews 3 and 4. Now, of course, this is an experience that God intends us to know increasingly in our lives,
but notice we are told, 'Let us therefore strive to enter that
rest' (Heb. 4: 11).

Furthermore, if a Christian needs simply to remain in a
passive state like a piece of clay in the hands of a potter, it is
difficult to see the purpose of the practical sections of the New
Testament. If it is simply a matter of 'letting Christ live out
His life in us', where is the place for injunctions like 'Look
carefully then how you walk' (Eph. 5: 15)? And what about

---

[1] D. M. Lloyd-Jones, *Christ our Sanctification* (IVF, 1948), p. 18.
[2] This is the picture we are given of the Christian life in *Pilgrim's
Progress*. There is very little suggestion there that it is simply a matter of
ceasing from struggling and striving. Christian had to face Giant Despair in Doubting Castle, to fight with Apollyon and to climb the hill
called Difficulty, to mention just a few of his experiences.

Paul's description of his own life: 'I press on toward the goal'
(Phil. 3: 14)? Remember, as we have already observed, that
the verb here is a word used for an athlete, straining every
nerve to reach the winning-post. One of the purposes of the
New Testament is to give us high and lofty motives to stimulate us to greater effort in the life of holiness: 'Since we have
these promises, beloved,' writes the apostle, 'let us cleanse ourselves from every defilement of body and spirit, and make
holiness perfect in the fear of God' (2 Cor. 7: 1). No, there are
no short cuts to victory in the New Testament, nor secret
formulae to be discovered. Rather, we need the whole range
of teaching which the Word of God gives us if we are to make
progress in sanctification. Holiness does not come in a moment,
but as the line of a well-known hymn expresses it, we must
'take time to be holy'.

PIETISM

This brings us to the opposite emphasis, pietism, but its label
is not as appropriate as 'quietism' is for the views we have just
been considering. The name is usually connected with the
movement in eighteenth-century Germany which came as a
protest against the dead orthodoxy of the Lutheran church of
the time. It had many admirable features, such as the growth
of Bible study groups. Its main concern was to emphasize the
need for practical Christianity, and it stressed the uselessness of
belief which does not lead to good works. The word 'pietism'
has come to be used by theologians for an emphasis on diligence in practical Christianity, and an insistence on self-
discipline and spiritual exercises.

Nevertheless, it is surely possible to discern a danger in it
every bit as harmful as that in unbalanced quietism. With an
over-emphasis on effort, a Christian could easily forget that it
is God who sanctifies, and that a Christian must rest believingly
on God and all His promises. When he fails in his efforts he
may well be left in despair, while any degree of success may
be taken as ground for self-congratulation instead of as an

opportunity for glorifying God. It is true that God has given everything to us in Christ, but this does not mean that after His initial saving He leaves man to purify himself. When we are told to work out our own salvation, we are immediately assured that God works in us (Phil. 2: 12 f.) and this word is in the present tense. We may stress the importance of practical Christianity and declare with James, 'Faith by itself, if it has no works, is dead' (Jas. 2: 17). But, at the same time, 'Without faith it is impossible to please him' (Heb. 11: 6).

MAINTAINING THE BALANCE

As in so many questions we are faced here with two sets of complementary truths, and error lies in neglecting one side or the other. Let T. C. Hammond summarize our position: 'While the New Testament emphasizes most emphatically that the work of grace is of God and not of our inherent capacity and so far lends support to the quietist position, it is equally emphatic on the fact that God worketh in us or with us and thus does justice to the truth resident in pietism. By combining both ideas it corrects the errors resident in both quietism and pietism.'[1] As we have seen repeatedly in this chapter, this balance of truth is carefully maintained in Scripture. Look, for example, at 2 Peter 1. In verses 3 and 4, the apostle emphasizes all that God has done for us to guarantee our sanctification: 'His divine power has granted to us all things that pertain to life and godliness, through the knowledge of him who called us to his own glory and excellence, by which he has granted to us his precious and very great promises, that through these you may escape from the corruption that is in the world because of passion, and become partakers of the divine nature.' However, it does not end there, for Peter goes on to give a list of virtues over which the Christian must show diligence. Here is what he says in verses 5–9: 'For this very reason make every effort to supplement your faith

[1] T. C. Hammond, *The New Creation* (Marshall, Morgan and Scott, 1953), p. 153.

with virtue, and virtue with knowledge, and knowledge with self-control, and self-control with steadfastness, and steadfastness with godliness, and godliness with brotherly affection, and brotherly affection with love. For if these things are yours and abound, they keep you from being ineffective or unfruitful in the knowledge of our Lord Jesus Christ. For whoever lacks these things is blind and short sighted and has forgotten that he was cleansed from his old sins.' The following verse shows one of the results of a Christian showing this diligence. He makes his 'calling and election sure' (verse 10, AV).

It may be asked how sanctification can still be the work of God when the Christian has to be so active in the pursuit of it. Surely the answer is given in words we have already quoted: 'God is at work in you, both to will and to work for his good pleasure' (Phil. 2: 13). The Christian is active because God stimulates him to effort and diligence, and impresses upon his conscience the encouragements and warnings of Scripture. So the person who truly believes the gospel with all its provisions for man's need and looks to Jesus, 'the pioneer and perfecter of our faith', will find himself challenged to 'run with perseverance the race that is set before us' (Heb. 12: 1 f.). The paradox is one with which we are continually being faced in the Christian life. We must be challenged to continued effort, but effort based on complete confidence in the sufficiency of Jesus Christ. It is well expressed in the familiar words:

> 'Fight the good fight with all thy might;
> Christ is thy strength, and Christ thy right.'

INCENTIVES

Nowhere do we see the relationship between faith and effort finding more practical expression than in the matter of incentives. This is the Bible's characteristic way of promoting holiness. It is not so much a matter of whispering in the ear of the Christian secret formulae or easy short cuts that bypass effort, but rather of setting before him incentives to stir him to endeavour in every department of his Christian life. Any system of teaching on holiness that does not find a prominent place for incentives is very deficient according to scriptural standards.

We had a basic example of this in chapter II, for we saw there that the holiness of God is the great stimulus to the Christian's holy living. The command 'You shall be holy' is enforced by the sublime truth 'I am holy'. We find frequent incentives in the connection between doctrine and practice in the Epistles. Look, for example, at Ephesians 4: 1, the verse which links together the doctrinal and practical sections of that Epistle. After the reader has gazed at the great panorama of Christian truth and all the blessings of the gospel that belong to him in the first three chapters, the practical matters of the remaining three chapters are introduced with a call to live up to the great facts he has had before him. 'I therefore, a prisoner for the Lord, beg you to lead a life worthy of the calling to which you have been called.'

There will be a number of other incentives in the remaining chapters of this book for which the reader should be on the look-out. In the meantime, see the relevance of incentives to the theme of this chapter, for incentives depend for their constraining power on the extent to which they are believed. The stronger the faith by which they are held the stronger their compulsion on a Christian's life. This is why, when a Christian grows, it is, amongst other things, in his faith.[1] This undoubtedly was a driving force in Paul's life. 'We have the same spirit of faith', he writes, 'as he had who wrote, "I believed, and so I spoke"' (2 Cor. 4: 13).

[1] See pp. 75 f.

CHAPTER XII

THE CHRISTIAN'S ENEMIES

A YOUNG Christian soon discovers that the Christian life is a conflict. He finds in the Word of God a clear pattern of the life that God wants him to live, but there are forces which are constantly drawing him in the opposite direction. While on the one hand he strives to follow the example of his Master, there seems to be a power that is always dragging him down, and again and again he performs actions, speaks words and thinks thoughts that afterwards he regrets and is even ashamed of. Now, he need not be surprised that his Christian life is like this because the Bible frequently describes it as such. The man who is 'following after holiness' will rally to the call of the Captain: 'Fight the good fight of the faith' (1 Tim. 6: 12). He must wrestle 'against the spiritual hosts of wickedness in the heavenly places' (Eph. 6: 12).

Now if we are to be victorious in this conflict, one of the first things we must do is to find out all we can about the enemy, and as we might expect, the Bible gives us plenty of information about this. We discover that the enemy is three-fold and usually denoted by the well-known trinity, 'the world, the flesh and the devil'.

I. THE DEVIL

This is the ultimate enemy with which we have to reckon and the Bible never underestimates his formidable nature and intention. His aim is nothing short of our complete destruction and ruin. He is the thief who 'comes only to steal and kill and destroy' (Jn. 10: 10). He is given a variety of names in Scripture, such as 'Satan', which means literally 'the adversary', 'the evil one' and 'the god of this world' (2 Cor. 4: 4), to mention just a few. When speaking of his strength, the Bible likens him to a 'roaring lion', who 'prowls around . . . seeking some one to devour' (1 Pet. 5: 8). So it is 'the power of Satan' (Acts 26: 18) from which men need to be delivered.

However, we are confronted not only by devilish power, but also by a subtle, scheming mind behind that power. The Bible uses another picture which likens him to a serpent, who is 'more subtle than any other wild creature' (Gn. 3: 1). He 'deceived Eve by his cunning' (2 Cor. 11: 3). He employs 'designs' (2 Cor. 2: 11) and 'wiles' (Eph. 6: 11—a word which Moffatt translates 'stratagems'). Indeed the Bible represents him as the supreme example of a depraved mind. He is, in short, to use our Lord's words, 'the father' of falsehood (Jn. 8: 44). He is able to use man to bring about his ends (e.g., Acts 13: 10), and can even fill the heart of a professed believer (Acts 5: 3). Probably one of his master-strokes is when he 'disguises himself as an angel of light' (2 Cor. 11: 14).

However, this is not all. Although the Bible gives an un-compromising picture of his strength and subtlety, the devil's power is not unlimited. We have a very telling picture in the first chapter of the book of Job, where the curtain is drawn aside and we are given a glimpse into heaven at the eternal realities lying behind the conflicts of this world. Here we see Satan having to gain permission from God before he can go and tempt Job. Paul also tells us that there is a limit placed upon the temptations to which a Christian is subjected (1 Cor. 10: 13). He is the foe that has already been defeated by Jesus and his ultimate destruction is sure and certain. Every time the gospel is preached in power we have an assurance that this is his ultimate fate (Lk. 10: 18), and we can be assured that 'the God of peace will soon crush Satan under your feet' (Rom. 16: 20).

To summarize, 'The witness of the New Testament then is clear. Satan is a malignant reality, always hostile to God and to God's people. But he has already been defeated in Christ's life and death and resurrection, and this defeat will become obvious and complete in the end of the age.'[1]

[1] L. Morris, *The New Bible Dictionary* (IVF, 1962), p. 1147.

II. THE WORLD

There are also two other factors that we have to take account of, and these may be regarded as the positions that the devil takes up.

One of these is the world, and it is significant that the devil is described as 'the god of this world' (2 Cor. 4: 4), and 'the ruler of this world' (Jn. 12: 31; 14: 30; 16: 11). This present world has become temporarily occupied by the enemy; the devil offered Christ all the kingdoms of this world assuming that they belonged to him already (Mt. 4: 8 f.). This is certainly how the Bible always speaks of the world in its present condition. 'We know', writes John, '. . . the whole world is in the power of the evil one' (1 Jn. 5: 19). This world is seen as opposed to God and it is out of it that Jesus came to redeem God's people.

What is the Christian's relationship to the world? To begin with, he has to live in it. Jesus prayed for His disciples: 'I do not pray that thou shouldst take them out of the world' (Jn. 17: 15), for it is in the world that a Christian is called upon to witness for Jesus Christ and to live the life that God has given him. It is in the world that a Christian is to be like salt, and like a light that is to 'shine before men' (Mt. 5: 13–16).

But not every Christian has obeyed his Lord in this matter, and there are those who imagine that they can keep their purity by living a life withdrawn from the world and its problems. It is true that many of the great saints of God, whose lives are recorded in the pages of Scripture, express the desire to be taken out of the world, including such illustrious men as David, Moses, Elijah and Jonah. In no case, however, was the request granted them; instead God gave them special strength to endure the circumstances which gave rise to their feelings. If we imagine that by monastic withdrawal we can avoid sin, we shall of course be disillusioned. The medieval monasteries bear plentiful witness to this, and perhaps it was this that prompted Thomas à Kempis to write: 'There is no order so holy, no place so secret, where there will be no temptation.'

In any case, God needs His people as witnesses. It is here in the world, right in the very midst of evil, that a Christian is called upon to exhibit the power of grace, to show forth his faith, courage and patience as a good soldier of Jesus Christ. He is called to be like Daniel in Babylon and the saints in Caesar's household.

At the same time, however, a Christian is never to regard himself as at home in the world. He is like an ambassador, who lives in an alien land and whose very calling demands that he should do so. But he is under the authority of another government to which he owes allegiance. 'Do not wonder, brethren, that the world hates you', wrote John (1 Jn. 3: 13), recalling no doubt the words of his Master which he had recorded (Jn. 15: 18). In the world a Christian is like a sojourner and a pilgrim (1 Pet. 1: 17; 2: 11), and a realization of this means that his life is going to be utterly different from those around him. Indeed, so opposed is the world to God that one cannot love both of them at once. A Christian who is at home in the world, follows all the world's fashions and accommodates his standards to those around him is in a very precarious condition indeed. He ought to heed seriously the words of John: 'If any one loves the world, love for the Father is not in him' (1 Jn. 2: 15), and the warning of James: 'Do you not know that friendship with the world is enmity with God?' (Jas. 4: 4). This is why a continual desire for worldly pleasures which are tainted by sin is often a sign that all is not well. Some of this world's pleasures, even in moderation, will undermine a Christian's spiritual life. If a married man wants to flirt with other girls, even in moderation, one assumes that there is something wrong with his marriage, or if not, that there soon will be. So the command is clear and uncompromising, 'Come out from them, and be separate from them, says the Lord, and touch nothing unclean; then I will welcome you' (2 Cor. 6: 17). We are to 'abstain from every form of evil' (1 Thes. 5: 22).

So a Christian has to be in the world but not of it. Here, then, is the complete quotation from the Lord's high-priestly prayer, giving both aspects of His will for His disciples: 'I do not pray that thou shouldst take them out of the world, but that thou shouldst keep them from the evil one' (Jn. 17: 15). Clearly, the Christian's is no easy course, and such an attitude is going to involve him in unending conflict. He will find himself right out in the middle of the stream, but often swimming against it and refusing to be carried along with the current. Nevertheless, as he realizes the privileges which are his, he will gladly endure the hardships and will be able to sing with John Newton:

> 'Saviour, since of Zion's city
> I, through grace, a member am,
> Let the world deride or pity,
> I will glory in Thy name.'

III. THE FLESH

This brings us to the third foe that we have to face, the flesh. And this is most relevant of all to the subject of sanctification, for it brings before us the solemn facts of our own nature with which the Holy Spirit comes to grips in sanctification.

We must begin by seeing clearly what the Bible means by this word. The Greek word is *sarx* and it *can* refer simply to physical flesh. However, it usually has the deeper significance that we are considering here, especially in the writings of Paul.

a. The flesh is limited

This comes out fairly clearly in St. John's Gospel, where the limitation of one who has only been 'born of the flesh' (Jn. 3: 6) is that he 'cannot enter the kingdom of God' (Jn. 3: 5). The flesh is of no avail, especially in the things that pertain to the spirit, beyond its own sphere. 'It is the spirit that gives life, the flesh is of no avail' (Jn. 6: 63). As an example of this we have what Jesus pointed out to Peter just after he had confessed that He was the Christ, 'Flesh and blood has not revealed this to you' (Mt. 16: 17). To understand the truth about Christ's Person demands something more than the natural faculties, the physical brain.

b. The flesh is weak

Here, an obvious example to quote is what Jesus said in the Garden of Gethsemane, 'The spirit indeed is willing, but the flesh is weak' (Mt. 26: 41). Peter, with all his promises of loyalty, was easily overcome by fatigue. Sometimes the expression, 'all flesh', is used to refer to the human race as a whole, especially in its present need and weakness in contrast to God's power. The psalmist boasts that because he has put his trust in God, 'What can flesh do to me?' (Ps. 56: 4). Jesus, in His high-priestly prayer, was able to claim that He had been given 'power over all flesh' (Jn. 17: 2).

It is because of the weakness of the flesh that law alone cannot produce salvation. As the apostle writes, God has done for us in Christ 'what the law, weakened by the flesh, could not do' (Rom. 8: 3). Indeed, Paul is able to say, 'I delight in the law of God, in my inmost self' (Rom. 7: 22). He was able to recognize the truth and righteousness of God's law. What lay between this and the actual putting into practice of that law was the weakness of his own fleshly nature.

c. The flesh is the gateway for sin

Paul brings this out very clearly, amongst other things, when he describes sin as 'another law at war with the law of my mind and making me captive to the law of sin which dwells in my members' (Rom. 7: 23). Sin can take the perfectly natural and God-created functions of the body and turn them into 'the lusts of the flesh'. Eating and drinking can be turned into gluttony. Sex can find its expression in adultery, fornication and other ways of dishonouring the body. While sleep can become sloth. These are examples of what happens when we allow sin to 'reign in (our) mortal bodies, to make (us) obey their passions' (Rom. 6: 12).

d.   The body is morally neutral

However, we must never fall into the error of supposing that the body is evil in itself. This error has led to two opposite and extreme views. On the one hand, the idea that the body is inherently evil and beyond redemption has led to unrestrained licence, while on the other, it has led to extremes in unavailing asceticism. Both, of course, are quite contrary to Scripture. There is no room here to go into the various doctrines which refute this idea, such as the fact that God has created our bodies, the incarnation which shows that flesh is not necessarily evil, and the future redemption of the body. What concerns us here, however, is to notice that the body is capable of sanctification. The flesh may be defiled, it is true (Jude 8), but notice that it can also be purified (Heb. 9: 13). Paul declares that it is God's purpose to 'sanctify you wholly', and in this he goes on to include 'your spirit and soul *and body*' (1 Thes. 5: 23). Just as a Christian must live 'in the world', so must he also live 'in the flesh'. Alongside all the privileges that come to the Christian from the glorious truth of the indwelling Christ, Paul still describes the present life of the Christian as 'the life I now live in the flesh' (Gal. 2: 20). Indeed, the body is even described as 'a temple of the Holy Spirit' (1 Cor. 6: 19). We, for our part, are exhorted: 'present your bodies as a living sacrifice' (Rom. 12: 1).

e.   The flesh and the mind are in conflict

From the description that Paul gives of the battlefield in Romans 7, we see that there are other factors at work. There is the law of God which appeals to his mind. He is able to claim, 'I delight in the law of God, in my inmost self' (Rom. 7: 22), and he has already given his assessment of it in an earlier verse, 'So the law is holy, and the commandment is holy and just and good' (Rom. 7: 12). Indeed, the whole conflict is summarized in the final verse of the chapter: 'So then, I of myself serve the law of God with my mind, but with my flesh I serve the law of sin' (Rom. 7: 25). It is between these two that he finds himself torn.

It would, however, be a mistake to imagine that sin restricts its activities to the realm of the flesh. Rather its aim is to capture the mind as well. So Paul can speak of the 'carnal mind' (see Rom. 8: 5 ff.) and the 'sensuous mind' (Col. 2: 18). A person in this condition will 'walk after the flesh', for here is a life in which the flesh is uppermost and dominates not only the actions but even the thinking that underlies them. This is how Paul describes Gentile Christians before their conversion, when he looks back to the time 'we all once lived in the passions of our flesh, following the desires of body and mind, and so we were by nature children of wrath, like the rest of mankind' (Eph. 2: 3).

This, of course, was a very fair description of life in a typical Greek city. There they had no centuries of Christian tradition to influence their social conventions and respectability. Are there not increasing signs that society is reverting to this situation today? The spiritual and moral capital on which we have been living for so many years is now beginning to wear thin, and the life of those around us is more and more dominated by 'the lusts of the flesh'.

The issues are clear and plain in this picture of the battlefield and the foes that we face. How, then, do we fight against them?

CHAPTER XIII

MORTIFICATION

ALTHOUGH the actual word 'mortify' comes only twice in the New Testament, it is a useful one to study, because it gets right to the heart of the conflict in which the Christian is involved, and which is such an essential part of his sanctification. It means that we are not merely fighting against temptation as an external foe, but are facing the realities of sin in our own nature. Two verses show this:

> 'If you live according to the flesh you will die, but if by the Spirit you put to death the deeds of the body you will live' (Rom. 8: 13).
> 'Put to death therefore what is earthly in you' (Col. 3: 5).

There are in fact two different words used for 'mortify' in these two verses, but there is no need to look for varying shades of meaning. Both of them mean 'to exterminate life' or 'to put to death'. They speak of a violent contest and may be compared to the cutting off of hands and plucking out of eyes that offend in Mark 9: 43 ff. Notice, too, that it is a continuous activity, for the use of the present tense in both these verses implies that mortification is something a Christian must always be doing. Just as the principle of indwelling sin never ceases in this life to be a constant problem to the believer, so mortification is always incumbent upon him. Well might John Owen say: 'He who ceases from this duty, lets go all endeavours after holiness.'[1] So, as the same writer continues a few pages later, 'We must be exercising it every day, and in every duty. Sin will not die, unless it be constantly weakened. Spare it, and it will heal its wounds, and recover its strength. We must continually watch against the operations of this principle of sin: in our duties, in our calling, in conversation,

---

[1] J. Owen, *On the Holy Spirit* (1674), p. 307.

in retirement, in our straits, in our enjoyments, and in all that we do. If we are negligent on any occasion, we shall suffer by it; every mistake, every neglect is perilous.'[1] How then do we mortify the sinful nature within us?

THE FUNCTION OF GOD'S LAW

To begin with, we must appreciate the part that God's law plays in all this. In Romans 7[2] Paul deals with God's law in relation to our sanctification, and, which is just as important, shows us what God's law cannot do.

In verses 7–13, Paul shows what this meant before he became a Christian. Then in verse 14 there is a significant change of tense from the past to the present, as Paul goes on to show what it meant to him as a Christian. Paul was not speaking of any lower state of Christian experience which he had left behind. He was writing as one who had learnt to 'delight in the law of God, in my inmost self' (verse 22), a law which he described as 'holy, and the commandment is holy and just and good' (verse 12). Paul is here writing out of a mature experience of God's grace. As Bishop Handley Moule observed: 'He who can truly speak thus of an inmost sympathy, a sympathy of delight, with the most holy law of God, is no half-Christian; certainly not in St. Paul's view of things.'[3]

What the law cannot do

Much as we may glory in God's law, however, we must never lose sight of its limitations. Not that there is anything inadequate about God's law in itself; it is in men that the inadequacy lies—to use Paul's words, it was 'weakened by the flesh' (Rom. 8: 3). Because of this, a set of rules, even

[1] J. Owen, *On the Holy Spirit* (1674), p. 310.
[2] A careful study of this and the surrounding chapters of Romans would be a great aid to understanding this entire theme, especially with the help of J. R. W. Stott's most enlightening exposition of these chapters in *Men Made New* (IVF, 1966).
[3] H. C. G. Moule, *The Epistle to the Romans* (Pickering and Inglis, 1956), p. 192.

though coming from God Himself, can neither justify nor sanctify. We will look at both of these limitations in turn.

1. In *Pilgrim's Progress*, Christian very early in his journey discovered that the law cannot justify. He learnt this the hard way, foolishly following Mr. Worldly Wiseman's advice, and turning away from the road he had been treading, to call at Mr. Legality's house on Mount Sinai. Here is what happened: 'So Christian turned out of his way to go to Mr. Legality's house for help; but, behold, when he was got now hard by the hill, it seemed so high, and also that side of it that was next the wayside did hang so much over, that Christian was afraid to venture further, lest the hill should fall on his head; wherefore there he stood still, and wotted not what to do. Also his burden now seemed heavier to him as he set him again on the right road. "No man was as yet ever rid of his burden by him; no, nor ever is like to be: ye cannot be justified by the works of the law".' No, a set of rules, even when given by God Himself, cannot make a person acceptable with God. 'A man is not justified by works of the law' (Gal. 2: 16).

2. The apostle asserts that the law cannot sanctify either; it can have even the opposite effect: 'But sin, finding opportunity in the commandment, wrought in me all kinds of covetousness. Apart from the law sin lies dead. I was once alive apart from the law, but when the commandment came, sin revived and I died' (Rom. 7: 8, 9). And so, through the weakness of human flesh, the very law of God Himself 'which promised life proved to be death to me' (Rom. 7: 10). There is something very realistic about this observation of Paul. A prohibition can indeed be very provocative, and the command 'Thou shalt not' can produce an irresistible urge to do the very thing it forbids; it can hardly be described as having a sanctifying effect!

Here is a further lesson which Christian in *Pilgrim's Progress* had to learn, and he did so through a superb illustration in Interpreter's House. He was taken into a large room which was full of dust. When a man began to sweep, the dust rose into the air and almost choked him. Before the room could be cleaned water had to be sprinkled to keep the dust down. Let Interpreter give his own explanation: 'This parlour is the heart of a man that was never sanctified by the sweet grace of the Gospel; the dust is his original sin, and inward corruptions, that have defiled the whole man. He that began to sweep at first, is the Law; but she that brought water, and did sprinkle it, is the Gospel. Now, whereas thou sawest, that so soon as the first began to sweep, the dust did so fly about that the room by him could not be cleansed, but that thou wast almost choked therewith; this is to show thee, that the law, instead of cleansing the heart (by its working) from sin, doth revive, put strength into, and increase it in the soul, even as it doth discover and forbid it, for it doth not give power to subdue.' So we can see how Paul could say, 'The power of sin is the law' (1 Cor. 15: 56), for unless accompanied by the gospel the law is precisely this.

Why the law is limited

Why is God's law unable to achieve either our justification or sanctification? The answer we give to this is no mere academic one, but is vital to a life of holiness. To use Paul's expression, the law was 'weakened by the flesh' (Rom. 8: 4). That is, there is nothing deficient in the law itself; the weakness is in us. Paul confessed his own bitter experience of this solemn fact in Romans 7: 14–25. Repeatedly he informs us that the law of God in which he delights he finds himself powerless to perform. This causes him to cry out in anguish, 'Wretched man that I am! Who will deliver me from this body of death?' (verse 24).

And Paul's burden is not made any lighter by what the law reveals of the seriousness of sin and its tragic consequences.

What the law can and must do

We can see now the important role which God's law must play in our sanctification. Although on its own it can never sanctify, nonetheless it provides us with one of the indispensable incentives for the mortification of our sinful natures. As H. W. Cragg commented, at the 1963 Keswick Convention, on this desperate cry of Paul: 'Paul has discovered something which is absolutely fundamental to holy living. He has discovered, I believe, that this outcry of distress is written into the very fabric of a holy life. It is not a crisis to pass; it is part of the very fabric of holiness. He never looked at himself without shame, from which he turns in loathing to look again on Christ.'[1] Here is one of the marks of growth in grace, not extravagant claims to victory, but a loathing of the sinful nature that remains.

J. R. W. Stott also has some very pointed comments on this, the main theme of Romans 7. 'Indeed, an honest and humble acknowledgment of the hopeless evil of our flesh, even after the new birth, is the first step to holiness. To speak quite plainly, some of us are not leading holy lives for the simple reason that we have too high an opinion of ourselves. No man ever cries aloud for deliverance who has not seen his own wretchedness. In other words, the only way to arrive at faith in the power of the Holy Spirit is along the road of self-despair. No device exists to settle this issue for good. The power and subtlety of the flesh are such that we dare not relax one moment. The only hope is unremitting vigilance and dependence.'[2]

'Load thy conscience with the guilt of it' is the attitude which John Owen demands towards our sin. 'Bring the holy law of God into thy conscience, lay thy corruption to it, pray that thou mayest be affected with it.'[3]

THE DEATH OF CHRIST—'ITS MERITORIOUS CAUSE'

Now the great fact on which we are to reckon is the death of Christ, which John Owen has called the 'Meritorious Cause' of our mortification. We have already seen that the offering of Christ is the only ground on which a person who

[1] H. W. Cragg, *The Keswick Week*, 1963, p. 51.
[2] J. R. W. Stott, *Men Made New* (IVF, 1966), p. 74.
[3] J. Owen, *Temptation and Sin* (Zondervan, 1959), pp. 56 f.

is defiled by sin can be set apart for God.[1] We are now concerned with its importance to mortification, because it has much to do with the Christian's attitude to his sin.

This is one of the principal themes of Romans 6: 1–14. The chapter begins with Paul anticipating a common objection to his gospel of free forgiveness and especially his expression of it in the closing two verses of chapter 5. Does this mean, he asks, that we can continue a life of sin because forgiveness is so easy? Indeed if, as he has just stated, 'where sin increased, grace abounded all the more', it would seem that the more we sin the more we experience God's grace.

Now a proper understanding of the death and resurrection of Christ and the believer's intimate relationship with them must result in an emphatic denial of such a suggestion. A Christian is in personal union with Christ, a state which is inwardly created by faith and outwardly signified by baptism, in which Christ's death is reckoned as the Christian's death. It is as if he himself had suffered death, the penalty for sin. Because of this, sin and its penalty has no further claim on him. Because such a person has shown the attitude of God towards his past sinful life, he can now regard this as a closed book.[2]

Now the relationship of all this to mortification is seen in the three logical steps of verse 6. The New English Bible translation is especially helpful here. 'We know that the man we once were has been crucified with Christ, for the destruction of the sinful self, so that we may no longer be the slaves of sin.' 'The man we once were' is a fitting rendering of 'our old man' (AV), for this can hardly be the same thing as 'the body of sin' (AV), which comes later in the same sentence. This expression, 'our old man', is used in the same sense in Colossians where it is used for the old pattern of life which the believer had followed in his pre-Christian days, and which it is assumed he has finished with. Holy living is

[1] See pp. 34 f.
[2] See J. R. W. Stott, *Men Made New* (IVF, 1966), p. 31 for a complete exposition of this passage.

demanded from a Christian on the assumption that he has 'put off the old nature with its practices' (Col. 3: 9). On what ground does Paul make this assumption? It is given in Romans 6: 6: 'Our old self was crucified with him.' The penalty for the old way of life has been fully paid by Christ, and the Christian when he believed Christ made that death his own.

Now, Paul goes on, the purpose of this was that 'the sinful body might be destroyed'. This does not mean that our sinful nature is completely eradicated as other occurrences of this word in the New Testament demonstrate. Rather its power is broken through the death of Christ. This in turn means 'that we may no longer be the slaves of sin' (NEB).

Since this is what happened to our sins when Christ died, in verse 11 we are told 'Consider yourselves dead to sin'. That is, we should accept the fact and live accordingly. Of course, there is a paradox here, and as F. F. Bruce points out: 'This apparent paradox is one that we meet repeatedly in the Pauline writings, where believers are enjoined time and again to be what they are—to be in actual practice what they are as members of Christ. Thus they are said to "have put off the old man with his deeds" and to "have put on the new man" (Col. 3: 9 f.), while elsewhere they are exhorted to "put off . . . the old man" and "put on the new man" (Eph. 4: 22, 24).'[1]

The word 'crucify' is used also of a Christian's policy towards sin's two allies, the flesh and the world:

> 'And those who belong to Christ Jesus have crucified the flesh with its passions and desires' (Gal. 5: 24).
> 'But far be it from me to glory except in the cross of our Lord Jesus Christ, by which the world has been crucified to me, and I to the world' (Gal. 6: 14).

Now it is true that in the first of these two examples the crucifying is something the Christian has done, rather than

[1] F. F. Bruce, *Romans* (Tyndale New Testament Commentary, 1963), p. 44.

something which has been done to him. The basic idea, however, is the same. Paul assumes by his use of the past tense that his readers, by virtue of their relation to Christ, have shared His attitude towards their sin, the flesh and the world in which they live. For a Christian to live a life dominated by the flesh or in fellowship with the world is a denial of his very relationship to a crucified Christ.

A Christian who is growing in his love for Jesus Christ is increasingly influenced by what his salvation cost. He is aware that he has been 'bought with a price' and is therefore under an obligation to 'glorify God in (his) body' (1 Cor. 6: 20). To state it the other way round, the more a Christian considers what his sin cost the Saviour, the more he will shrink from it. Again we are indebted to John Owen, 'Bring thy lust to the Gospel,—not for relief, but for further conviction of its guilt; look on Him whom thou hast pierced, and be in bitterness. Say to thy soul "What have I done? What love, what mercy, what blood, what grace have I despised and trampled on! Is this the return I make to the Father for His love, to the Son for His blood, to the Holy Ghost for His grace?" '[1]

THE WAY OF MORTIFICATION

a. Negatively

Mortification involves a constant weakening of sin by refusing to give it any outlet and denying it any expression. This will apply to particular sins and the whole range of sin, remembering that the aim is 'that the sinful body might be destroyed' (Rom. 6: 6). It will also mean that we starve out our sinful nature by refusing to feed it on the food by which it flourishes: 'Let not sin therefore reign in your mortal bodies, to make you obey their passions' (Rom. 6: 12). Because of this a Christian must apply extreme care about how he feeds his mind, such as the books he reads and the conversations he listens to.

[1] J. Owen, *Temptation and Sin* (Zondervan, 1959), p. 58.

We must never fall into the error of imagining that this is an easy undertaking. There is a realism in the description of John Owen: 'Some look upon it as an easy task. But is it for nothing that the Holy Spirit expresses it by mortification, or killing? Certainly this intimates a violent contest. Everything will do its utmost to preserve its life. Let no man think to kill sin with a few gentle strokes. He, who has once smitten the serpent, if he follow not his blow till it be slain, may repent that ever he began the quarrel; and so will he who undertakes to deal with sin, if he pursue it not constantly to death; sin will revive, and the man must die.'[1]

We ought to notice that, despite what some have taught, there is nothing harmful in this attitude towards our sinful nature. It is far removed from repression, of which psychologists have warned us. The latter involves a refusal to face even the possibility of sin. 'I am not the kind of person to do that, because I am not tempted in that way' expresses an attitude of repression. Mortification means that a Christian says, 'I am the kind of person who can do that very sin, but by the grace of God I will not do it.'

At the very heart of mortification is the denial of self. Here, of course, we get to the very heart of sin. It is rebellion against God, putting self on the throne of one's life instead of Him. It is self that spoils people's lives again and again and can be intruded into all kinds of religious activity. How often Christian fellowship has been marred and ruined by petty squabbling, which has uncrucified self at the bottom of it. Such strife and division were the symptoms of the carnality of the Corinthian Christians (1 Cor. 3: 3). Little wonder that Jesus enjoins any would-be disciple, 'Let him deny himself' (Mt. 16: 24).

b. Positively

The Bible always encourages a Christian to be positive, and this certainly applies in the matter of mortification: 'Walk by the Spirit, and do not gratify the desires of the flesh' (Gal.

[1] J. Owen, On The Holy Spirit (1674), p. 311.

5: 16). As a Christian lives in fellowship with the Holy Spirit of God, and fosters in his life the things that please Him, so the less worthy things are crowded out of his life. Or, as J. R. W. Stott puts it, mortification is to be accompanied by aspiration.[1] So the way to mortify sin is both to 'starve it out' and 'crowd it out'. John Owen calls this 'the weakening of the flesh by the growth of positive graces', and he observes that every sin has a corresponding virtue by which it can be displaced. He continues: 'So by the implanting and growth of humility is pride weakened, passion by patience, uncleanness by purity of mind and conscience, love of this world by heavenly-mindedness.'[2] There is a very useful biblical exposition of this in Ephesians 4: 22–32, where the apostle gives a list of what we are to 'put off' and side by side with it a list of corresponding virtues to 'put on'. For example, a Christian is not only to refrain from stealing, but in its place 'Let him labour, doing honest work with his hands, so that he may be able to give to those in need' (verse 28). In other words, a Christian is not just to be satisfied with earning enough to make it unnecessary to steal, but he is to aim at being in a position to give to others.

One of the ways in which a Christian can be positive is in the way that he feeds his thought life, 'As he thinketh in his heart, so is he' (Pr. 23: 7, AV). The very opposite of a carnal Christian is one who is dominated by his mind and not by his flesh, and has a mind that is filled with what is lovely. We have, of course, the well-known advice of the apostle Paul in this connection: 'Finally, brethren, whatever is true, whatever is honourable, whatever is just, whatever is pure, whatever is lovely, whatever is gracious, if there is any excellence, if there is anything worthy of praise, think about these things' (Phil. 4: 8).

THE HOPE OF VICTORY

In order to be realistic about the Christian life, it has been

[1] J. R. W. Stott, *Men Made New* (IVF, 1966), pp. 91f.
[2] J. Owen, *Temptation and Sin* (Zondervan, 1959), p. 32.

necessary to emphasize again and again the severity of the conflict in which a Christian is involved, the subtlety of the foe that he faces and the extreme difficulty of the mortification that God commands him to undertake. However, we must not imagine that this is inevitably a hopeless struggle. Satan may indeed be a subtle and deadly foe but we must never lose sight of the promise that 'Where sin increased, grace abounded all the more' (Rom. 5: 20), and the defiant cry, 'if God is for us, who is against us?' (Rom. 8: 31). The fight of the Christian against the world, the flesh and the devil is not to be likened to the hopeless struggle of the unregenerate man, who is still under the bondage of sin. The Christian certainly has to fight sin day by day, and sometimes it will get the better of him, but this is not the same thing as letting 'sin ... reign in your mortal bodies, to make you obey their passions' (Rom. 6: 12). The devil is already a defeated foe and his doom has been settled once and for all by the death and resurrection of Jesus Christ. So that if we undertake the mortification of sin, relying on all the resources that God places at our disposal, in other words, if we do it 'by the Spirit', we have the assurance of God's Word, 'you will live' (Rom. 8: 13).

CHAPTER XIV

THE END OF THE WAY

THE way of holiness will not go on for ever; one day it will end. The process of sanctification will then be complete. The fight will be over and the Christian's enemies completely destroyed. This will be when this life is ended and when the course of history reaches its consummation at the second coming of Christ. Most of God's people enter this, the final stage in their salvation, through death. Those who are still alive at Christ's coming will also be transformed and glorified.

GLORIFICATION

What will all this mean for the Christian? The word often used is 'glorification', and it is important to understand its relationship to present sanctification. In one sense it is the final stage in sanctification. Negatively, the mortification of sin will be complete and sin will be finally uprooted from the Christian's nature, for he will be 'without blemish' (Jude 24). Positively, the Christian will be 'like him' (1 Jn. 3: 2). The conforming to the image of God's Son will then be accomplished, and this is the goal towards which the present sanctifying activity of the Holy Spirit is working.

Another way of putting it is to say that the distinction we carefully drew in chapter VII between justification and sanctification will then no longer apply. This is what some well-known words of Hooker virtually amount to: 'The righteousness wherewith we shall be clothed in the world to come is both perfect and inherent; that whereby we are here justified is perfect but not inherent; that whereby we are sanctified, inherent, but not perfect.' It is surely clear from this that one of the errors of perfectionism lies in confusing sanctification and glorification. Entire sanctification is certainly taught in Scripture but it will not be realized until the coming of Jesus Christ. This is clearly taught in some words of the apostle Paul, 'May the God of peace himself sanctify you wholly; and may your spirit and soul and body be kept sound and blameless at the coming of our Lord Jesus Christ' (1 Thes. 5: 23).

Another mistake is to separate these two doctrines. Sanctification, we are sometimes told, is salvation from the power of sin, whereas glorification will be salvation from the presence of sin. But this could be a misleading half-truth. As we have already seen, sanctification does not merely consist in keeping the sinful nature under control, although it certainly includes that. Rather, it involves an inward work of the Holy Spirit whereby we are being transformed into the very likeness of Christ, and our inward sinful nature is being mortified. It is the very process of which glorification is the final stage.

The Bible often uses the word 'salvation' for this, and the verb 'save' in the future tense (see, *e.g.*, Mt. 24: 13). Looking forward to that great day, Paul says, 'Salvation is nearer to us now than when we first believed' (Rom. 13: 11). When Christ comes again, 'Unto them that look for him shall he appear the second time without sin unto salvation' (Heb. 9: 28, AV). As E. M. B. Green commented when speaking at the Keswick Convention in 1964: 'Sometimes we sing hymns about full salvation. This is not true. We have not got full salvation now. That belongs to the future.'[1]

This salvation will involve the complete defeat of all the Christian's enemies. Instead of the sinful world in which the Christian has now to live, there will be 'new heavens and a new earth in which righteousness dwells' (2 Pet. 3: 13). As for the devil himself, he will be thrown into the lake of fire (Rev. 20: 10), while the Christian, to use the words of the Prayer Book Burial Service, will be delivered from 'the burden of the flesh'. No longer will the Christian be dragged

---

[1] E. M. B. Green, *The Keswick Week*, 1964, p. 131.

down by the weakness of his flesh. In *Pilgrim's Progress* we see Christian and Hopeful, after passing through the river of death, climbing up the hill towards the Celestial City with ease. No longer is there the toil and the striving which they had known during their earthly pilgrimage, because now 'they had left their mortal garments behind them in the river'. Not that we look forward to a disembodied state, but rather to the possession of a body which is to be glorified and completely freed from the limitations and the weakness of our mortal flesh (see 1 Cor. 15: 50–52; 2 Cor. 5: 1–5).

THE BLESSED HOPE

A word that is frequently used in connection with the final consummation of our salvation is 'hope'. Not only does a Christian look back to the cross, and upward to Christ on the throne, but he also looks forward to the day when he will stand before Him. So, as Paul puts it, 'in this hope we are saved' (Rom. 8: 24), and he describes the event itself as 'our blessed hope' (Tit. 2: 13). Now the common usage of this word does not convey at all its biblical meaning. It is often used to express uncertainty, and the expression, 'I hope so', immediately conveys an impression of doubt. Nothing could be further removed from the meaning of this word in the Bible, for there it expresses complete certainty. Where the sanctifying work of the Holy Spirit is proceeding in a Christian's life, he can be absolutely sure that that work will be completed. Here is the confidence that Paul expressed to the Philippians, 'And I am sure that he who began a good work in you will bring it to completion at the day of Jesus Christ' (Phil. 1: 6). The verse from 1 Thessalonians 5 about entire sanctification, which we have already quoted, is followed by the assurance, 'He who calls you is faithful, and he will do it' (1 Thes. 5: 24). Here is further evidence that just as it is impossible to separate sanctification from justification, so it is impossible to separate it from glorification. Those in whose lives God is now at work can be quite sure that this will not be left incomplete. God's work is never an unfinished symphony.

This means that the present work of the Holy Spirit is a guarantee of its completion. Indeed, Paul refers to the Holy Spirit as 'the earnest of our inheritance', for the Greek word for 'earnest' was used for a deposit or first instalment of a payment pledging more to follow. Here we have one of the greatest incentives to holy living during this life. Material things are only temporary and the world and the flesh with all their apparent pleasures will pass away. Holy living is the only pursuit really worth following. 'Since all these things are thus to be dissolved, what sort of persons ought you to be in lives of holiness and godliness' (2 Pet. 3: 11) is the sober advice of Peter. The prospect of what we shall be like on that great day encourages us to work towards it, and to co-operate with the Holy Spirit in His present operation in our lives. 'Every one who thus hopes in him', wrote John, 'purifies himself as he is pure' (1 Jn. 3: 3).

> 'Work on, then, Lord, till on my soul
>   Eternal light shall break,
> And, in Thy likeness perfected,
>   I "satisfied" shall wake.'

E.H.H.